Praise

"Within the young adult cancer community, we hold no one's disease above anyone else's. Katie Campbell is the embodiment of that humility and strength who sheds light on the invisibility of our stories amongst the noise of pink ribbons and "finding a cure.""

MATTHEW ZACHARY
Young Adult Cancer Survivor, Founder/CEO, Stupid Cancer

"Katie Campbell's desire to continue living is so powerful she is unwilling to forgo any option to attain that goal. This desire radiates in her writing, leaving her readers both inspired and absolutely positive that Campbell is the world's biggest badass."

BENJAMIN RUBENSTEIN
Author of the Cancer-Slaying Super Man Books

"I commend Katie for her courage to share her story to help other young breast cancer survivors. Through my own journey with breast cancer I found loving yourself is hard when you feel like your body has failed you, however I agree with Katie that our bodies are incredible machines capable of taking us on great adventures. This is a nice book to remind all of us survivors about practicing acceptance, being vulnerable, and loving ourselves. Thanks Katie!"

JENNIFER MERSCHDORF
Diagnosed with breast cancer at age 36
& CEO of Young Survival Coalition

"The Courage Club is a brave friend when the most important things in life are taken away. Katie Campbell shows how letting go of what we expected, creates strength to embrace life and to live with everything we have."

DAVID FUEHRER
Young adult cancer survivor, Stupid Cancer Board of Directors

---

"Campbell inspires and empowers readers to live well. She is a ray of light."

EMILY DRAKE
Health Promotion Specialist, *EmilyDrake.ca*

the Courage club

A RADICAL GUIDE
TO AUDACIOUSLY
LIVING BEYOND CANCER

Katie A. Campbell

difference press

COPYRIGHT

DISCLAIMER

Cover & Interior Design: Heidi Miller

Editing: Cynthia Kane

Author's photo courtesy of Beryl Ayn Young

Dedication

For Andrew, my best friend, my pooks, my everything.
So lucky that you have been mine. I will always be yours.

For Gus and Donna, for your love. By never being a
helicopter you taught me how to take flight.

For Andy, for your unconditional love.
You'll never stop making me proud.

For Meredith, Jake, Mary, Tim, Matt, Jess, Angela,
Marci, Beth, Caitlin and Lo, for your friendship.
You have filled my life with love.

For my entire support system but especially Carl, Fran,
Ani and Kabir. You have carried us further than we
could ever have gone on our own.

For Dave Wilson and David Denton, who helped
make this book possible, and for David's love:
"In every rainbow, I think of you, Nancy Denton-Perlman.
Your love is eternal. Big hugs, David."

For all of my fellow young adult cancer thrivers.
You are my heroes.

Table of Contents

Welcome to the Courage Club!

"The purpose of this glorious life is not simply to endure it but to soar, stumble and flourish as you learn to fall in love with existence. We were born to live, my dear, not to merely exist."

BECCA LEE

If you had asked me when I was thirty what gave my life meaning, my answer would have been easy: my husband, my job, my friends and family, and becoming a mother, someday. That was it for me. That was all I needed. And it made sense; I would expect most people's lists would look quite similar to this. But within a few short months, every one of these meaning-makers would be damaged or destroyed by a crisis that continues to this day.

Just a few months after my thirtieth birthday, I was diagnosed with cancer. I went through a year of treatments, only to have the cancer metastasize and become Stage 4 (the kind that is associated with words like "terminal" and "incurable"). Within a few years, I had lost the ability to become a mother; many of my relationships, including my marriage, had been severely strained; and my job had taken a backseat to my numerous and demanding health needs. So there I was, in my early thirties, facing a life-threatening disease, finding many of the things that had given my life meaning either damaged or completely destroyed. I didn't know how long I had left to live, but I knew that I could not go on living a life without meaning.

Thankfully, most people will not find themselves with a cancer diagnosis this early in life. Yet, many of us do face crises that threaten our meaning-makers. Divorce, death, illness, loss of a job or a career transition, even a mid-life crisis, can make us feel like we've lost our life's meaning. As we grow up, we are handed ideas and ideals about what life should have in store for us. We write our story down, punctuating all of the pieces that will make us feel like worthy and successful people. The problem, I realized, is that all of my punctuations, all of the things that made my life meaningful, were external to myself. They were all things that I could lose, things that could be taken from me at any moment. This meant that my life could lose meaning based on factors beyond my control. If I lost my husband, or my job, my friendships or my ability to become a mother, what would make my life meaningful? What would make me want to go on living?

I needed to answer that question, because in whatever time I had left I wanted to enjoy a deep, rich and meaningful existence. I was having far too many what-is-the-point-of-getting-out-of-bed days, and I knew my life would be far too short to spend the remainder of it in bed. So I began reading, and listening, and talking, and soaking up wisdom from every direction. Slowly but surely, I began to build my life again. I found completely new sources of meaning. This didn't mean that I threw all of my old meaning-makers out. They were still important, and in many ways, my connection to them was made even richer and more dynamic.

It was not an easy path, but it has been so worthwhile. Finding new meaning in my life continues to help me, not just to get out of bed every morning, but to live as boldly and audaciously as I can with the time I've got left.

This is where the courage comes in. Courage has little to do with surviving cancer, and everything to do with connection. To build a meaningful life requires courage because it requires connecting, first and foremost, with ourselves. I am the only thing in my life that I cannot lose. I am the one thing that cancer cannot take away from me. The elements required to create that connection are not always things we see as courageous. Practicing acceptance, being vulnerable, and loving ourselves are often associated with weakness. But in reality, each of these things is an act of courage. If they were easy, we would have done them already.

The magic of connecting with ourselves in a deep and

meaningful way means that next we can connect with our bodies on a deeper level, and, eventually, we can connect with our world — the place where our relationships, our careers, and our kids live. When we enter our world coming from a space of authentic self-love, acceptance, vulnerability, and mindfulness, it makes all the connections we form there that much more meaningful.

In this book, I will share experiences with facing down my crisis. I will share how I learned to connect with myself, even in my least lovable moments. And I will share how, eventually, I found a way to go from barely living to becoming audaciously alive.

At the end of the day, we all deserve to live this one life we've been given as deeply as we can. I invite you to join me in the Courage Club, a place where we know bravery because we have faced down our own demons; a place where we are ready and willing to do the work required to accept, love and understand ourselves; a place where we are committed to nourishing, moving and caring for the bodies that carry us through this life; and a place where we have enough love and courage to engage with our world in real and authentic ways that are true to ourselves. Once you enter the Courage Club there is no turning back — but once you discover what it means to be audaciously alive, you won't ever want to.

My Story

"We have to continually be jumping off cliffs, and developing our wings on the way down."

KURT VONNEGUT

The first inkling that my body might have a habit of self-sabotage came in May 2013, just before my thirtieth birthday. I had gone in for a routine physical and afterward, my doctor called to let me know that she thought I might have an auto-immune disease. While I'd physically been feeling fine, my blood work showed that my thyroid levels were off. I had antibodies that came with a diagnosis of Graves' disease, a form of hyperthyroidism in which the thyroid is over stimulated, sending your metabolism soaring.

For a few weeks I had no symptoms. And then one day, out of nowhere, Graves' came barging through like a runaway train. It felt as if something were pulling down on every muscle in my body. Standing up felt like performing a 200 lb. shoulder press. Walking a few feet was like running a marathon. Graves' had overtaken my body and had all my systems running so quickly that my body was both exhausted and starved. After a visit to Toronto for a good friend's wedding, I literally had to lie down in the security line at the airport on our return trip home because I could no longer stand. When I arrived back in DC, I quickly found an endocrinologist who prescribed medication, but I spent an entire month in bed waiting for the medicine to kick in.

From the beginning, I was deeply ashamed of my illness. I had been stricken with what felt like "out-of-shape lazy slob" disease. Merely sitting up sent my heart racing and took my breath away, so I spent most of the time trying not to move at all. The only time I did get up was to eat more food, to feed my insatiable hunger. I was so ashamed that I basically disappeared from my life for a month and told only my boss and my closest friends and family what was happening.

As I recovered from Graves' over the summer I was determined to become the healthy young woman I had once been. I started on a strict diet and exercise routine, began seeing a naturopath and took a range of supplements. That August, my family took a vacation to the Pacific Northwest and my husband, Andrew, and I tagged on a few extra days in Vancouver. After an exhilarating day exploring Granville Island Andrew and I returned to the apartment we'd rented, popped in a movie and opened a bottle of wine. We had just started "fooling around" when Andrew said, "Hey, is this a muscle?" I felt the spot on my upper right breast that he was referring to and discovered a rock hard spot, roughly the size of a golf ball. I immediately flew into a panic; irrationally furious that he would think this terrifyingly foreign lump was just a muscle. I stumbled out of bed, ran to the bathroom, stared at my chest, groped at the lump, and spiraled into a panic attack.

I didn't know what the lump was, but I knew it was bad. Eventually, we pulled out our laptops and began doing research. We learned that the vast majority of lumps, particularly in younger women, were benign. So I made an appointment with my primary care physician for the day after we got home and we attempted to console ourselves with the fact that the odds were very much in my favor.

My physician examined the lump with a vague look of concern and referred me to a breast center to receive a mammogram and an ultrasound. I watched the radiologist carefully as she eyed the ultrasound. "You're going to need a biopsy," she said. "...today." "So it's not just a cyst?" I asked hopefully. "It's not a cyst," she said. "I'll have them fit you in this afternoon."

The biopsy was excruciating. I held the radiologist's hand as tears of pain and fear rolled down my cheeks. By the end of the day, I had a nurse navigator and an appointment with a breast surgeon. They were not taking my case lightly, which told me that I shouldn't either.

The next week my husband and I went back to the breast center, where our worst fears were confirmed: I had Stage 2A triple negative breast cancer.

The majority of breast cancers have one of three known receptors, either for the hormones Estrogen (ER) or Progesterone (PR), or for a protein called HER2. For these types of cancers, the receptors can be targeted in order to treat the cancer and prevent its return. Triple negative breast cancer has none of these three known receptors (hence the triply gloomy sounding name). This makes it one of the most difficult forms of breast cancer to treat. Recurrence rates are twice as high as other breast cancers, it is usually much faster growing and more deadly, and is also much more likely to impact young women. Lucky me.

My tumor was too big to operate on, so instead, I would begin treatment with 16 rounds of chemotherapy over five months. My oncologists also recommended I participate in the clinical trial being offered at my hospital, which would add one additional drug to the standard chemo regimen. I agreed to the trial and spent the next few weeks undergoing a battery of tests to determine if I qualified.

Before starting chemo, I began fertility treatments. In an industry where the average patient is 67 years old, I was lucky that I had even been offered the chance to preserve my fertility. The fertility concerns of so many young adults are often ignored in the rush to begin treatment. The treatments included self-injections and daily trips to the doctor. Those first few weeks I basically lived in doctors' offices and hospitals. Everywhere I went, I got sad looks from nurses, patients, technicians and receptionists. One lamented, "Oh, I thought you were lost. You're too young to be here!" I agreed.

By early October 2013, roughly one month after my diagnosis, I started on chemo. I began with 12 weekly rounds of Taxol, along with an experimental drug. Every Friday, Andrew and I would lug our laptops, pillows, blankets, and food to the hospital, and I'd spend the day getting an infusion. Usually, by mid-day Saturday, I started to feel sick and by Sunday night, I felt awful. I took off Mondays and sometimes Tuesdays, but was usually back to work on Wednesdays and Thursdays, functioning almost like a normal human being.

That fall was not a fun one. All of my weekends and half of every week from October to December were spent feeling sick. My body also had a few dramatic reactions that kept us on our toes. There was a trip to the emergency room for what we thought was a heart attack but turned out to be a swelling of the lining around my heart, and a full body rash so horrifically itchy that I had to sleep covered in ice packs. I became menopausal overnight, which gave me an entirely new appreciation for the hot flashes I had witnessed in older women.

As I maneuvered through my new life filled with illness, baldness and trips to the emergency room, I kept a blog documenting it all. I had decided early on that I would not let cancer be like Graves' disease. I would not hide away, ashamed of being the "sick girl." I instinctively knew that I would need all the help I could get and I found that the best way to do that was to bring all of my friends and family on the journey with me.

More than anything, I was writing to keep myself sane. Putting down into words what I was going through helped me understand the chaos unfolding around me, and helped me to get in touch with the emotions it was bringing up for me. And by sharing as much information as I did, it helped to stave off the well-meaning but often ignorant, and sometimes hurtful, questions people wanted to ask. Happily, I began to find, as time went on, that the words I had written primarily for myself were having an impact on other people, and best of all, were helping other young adult cancer patients navigate the same tough terrain.

When the holidays rolled around, I was lucky enough to get a two-week break in my treatments. I got to feel good for Christmas and the New Year and reveled in what it was like to feel whole again, even for a brief time. When I returned from my break, I jumped right into four rounds of Adriamycin/Cytoxan (A/C), infused every other week. I'd heard horror stories about this drug and the havoc it can wreak on a body. It's so toxic that you can only get four doses of it ever, in your entire life, because of the damage it can cause to your heart. When it took me more than ten days to recover from the first dose, I understood how it had gotten its reputation.

Around the same time, I got news that the first 12 weeks of chemo had not shrunk the tumor, as we had all hoped it would. The news was particularly devastating because I had been told that an earlier scan showed that the tumor was shrinking. My oncologist would later explain that the second scan had been read incorrectly. It hadn't occurred to me that this was a possibility — that signs of my survival could be misread as easily as a traffic sign.

This news made me feel like the tremendous amount of pain I had suffered through was all for naught. That feeling, combined with this new, incredibly harsh drug that left me sick for 12 out of every 14 days, brought me to a point of near collapse. It felt as if my brain were completely and utterly broken. One morning, about eleven days after my last infusion, I woke up to the reality that I still felt miserably ill. I had been through eleven straight days of pounding headaches, nausea, burning eyes, aching muscles, mouth sores that were inches long and made every bite and sip excruciating, and an overwhelming weakness that had me bent over and shuffling anytime I needed to get up. I realized that I could not bear the thought of going through this for another month.

At first, my response was simply to burst into tears. Then I began screaming about how I couldn't keep doing this. The emotional pain building up inside was so overwhelming that I began to repeat, "I can't," over and over and over. I started shaking my head and repeating those words. Somehow it felt like a huge relief. I let my brain and all the hurt just turn off and I sat there, for over an hour, shaking my head and repeating those two words. While this reaction was beyond worrisome for Andrew, for me it felt like the only rational coping mechanism I could come up with in a time of absolutely soul-crushing pain. As it turned out, this would be the first of many trauma responses I would experience on my journey with cancer.

As the next few months wore on, I survived chemo — but not without many more episodes of serious "trauma brain," as I began calling it. The outbursts and breakdowns only heightened as I headed for surgery. Though I had no cancer in my left breast, a double mastectomy improved survival rates for patients with triple negative breast cancer, and so it had been decided relatively early on that I would undergo a double mastectomy. I had therefore been expecting it for some time, but was still terrified of the pain and consequences of having the middle of my body amputated. I imagined waking up feeling completely and utterly maimed and never truly recognizing my own body ever again.

When I awoke from surgery, I learned that they had found cancer in multiple lymph nodes, increasing my stage from Stage 2A to Stage 2B. I don't remember much of my recovery, as a result of all of the pain meds, but I do remember being lucky enough to have a hospital room packed with friends and family, and then a packed house for much of my recovery. My two best friends, my brother and his girlfriend, my parents, and my husband were all there for me. We played Cards against Humanity in the hospital and they bought me a box of vegan cupcakes to celebrate my return home. They made an impossibly sad and difficult thing so much more bearable — and that made me feel deeply loved and incredibly lucky.

About a month after surgery I went back to my oncologist for a follow-up visit. I was scheduled to begin radiation soon, and by my birthday in June I would be done with treatments. Radiation was supposed to be the "easiest" of the treatments and I was perfectly happy to have saved the easiest for last. While Andrew and I waited for the doctor, a resident came in to talk with us. She finished with her preliminary exam and as she prepared to leave she said, almost in passing, "The doctor will discuss the additional chemo you'll be needing when she comes in." I responded with a look of sheer horror that obviously surprised her. She mumbled a few more things and left as quickly as possible.

Andrew and I consoled ourselves with the fact that she had no idea what she was talking about. That was until my oncologist came in.

The chemo had hardly touched the tumor, she explained — and it had spread to my lymph nodes, as we knew. This wasn't a good sign. She'd consulted with all of the other oncologists in the hospital, and the decision was unanimous. They recommended more chemo: three more months. I could go home and think it over, she told me.

The tears started streaming before she left. When she closed the door, I crumpled into a ball on the floor.

For the next few days, the only thought I could process was that I wanted out of my life. I wanted to escape it. I didn't want to die, but I did not want to be living this life anymore. I was finished. I could not go on. I could not bear any more pain. I lay in bed and cried. I pulled the bottle of painkillers from my side drawer. I held them close to my chest. They were a reassurance for me that I could escape if I needed to. I remember thinking that if I just swallowed all of those pills I wouldn't have to keep going. Or if I swallowed some of the pills maybe someone would realize how insane this was, how much pain I was being put through, and they would rescue me from this life.

Eventually, my husband took the pills and made me call a suicide prevention hotline. By the end of the day, I had called my nurse to let her know I would go through with the additional rounds of chemo.

I survived the next three months of chemo with just a handful of trips to the emergency room and some pretty severe anemia. Fortunately, radiation was indeed a walk in the park compared to everything else I had been through. It was tedious to go in for treatment every day, but it was a far cry from chemo.

On my last day of treatment I spent the morning feeling completely and utterly triumphant. I was free. The cancer had been in remission since my double mastectomy and at this point I had no more treatments left, no more appointments. By the evening, I was a nervous wreck. I called Andrew from my overnight work retreat sobbing, afraid and confused. Everyone saw my cancer as "done" but I was still reeling from a year's worth of treatments. All I could do was cross my fingers that cancer wouldn't come back into my life.

I eventually found my way back to myself and my life post-cancer. I got more involved in the young adult cancer community. I went on many adventures that fall, travelling to three new countries, seeing incredible sights, and taking on physical challenges. By the time 2015 rolled around, I was ready to embrace a brand new year.

Of course, cancer had other plans.

As my husband and I were driving home from our Christmas vacation that winter, the car in front of us came to a screeching halt and Andrew slammed on the brakes. The seatbelt dug into my neck as I jolted forward. When I moved the seat belt out of the way to rub the spot that ached I found a pea-sized lump next to my right clavicle. My stomach sank. I nearly threw up.

As with the last lump I'd found, I made an appointment with my primary care physician, and had an ultrasound to rule out anything suspicious. The ultrasound led to a biopsy and the biopsy confirmed my greatest fear: the cancer had returned.

My oncologist informed me that this less-than-one-cm tumor in my lymph node now meant that I had Stage 4 cancer. A diagnosis of Stage 4 triple negative breast cancer comes with a life expectancy of 13 months. She believed that chemo would not help me. She also believed that my cancer was radiation resistant. She suggested surgery, but my surgeon said it was inoperable. My oncologist also explained that I didn't qualify for any clinical trials because the infected lymph node was too small to meet the vast majority of trial requirements.

Feeling hopeless and afraid, I decided to seek out second, third, fourth, fifth and sixth opinions. My incredible network of support rallied in a matter of days and connected me with world-renowned doctors, frequent flyer miles and everything else I needed to take a tour of the nation's best hospitals. In the end, I visited Cleveland Clinic, the University of Chicago, Johns Hopkins, Mass General, Dana Farber, the Mayo Clinic, Memorial Sloan Kettering, MD Anderson, and the University of North Carolina. Every doctor had the same thing to say: they couldn't recommend any treatment at this time, but if I waited a few months for it to spread to my organs I would qualify for a clinical trial.

By this point, I was in complete despair. I assumed, by the way all the doctors had talked about my cancer, that I would not make it through another year. I had just started to build back my life, and now it was being taken away again. Andrew and I became nearly inseparable, not wanting to miss another moment of whatever precious time we had left together. We slept every night holding on to one another, literally, for dear life.

Eventually, a friend from my young adult cancer community reached out. She told me about her experience: how she'd also been told there were no treatment options left for her. She told me about a doctor she'd found in New York. He'd come from Memorial Sloan Kettering, but now ran a private practice. He had a completely novel approach to cancer and was able to provide patients with cutting-edge treatments like immunotherapies, as well as many other nontraditional and alternative options. The catch, of course, was that because he was outside of the system, everything would have to be paid for out-of-pocket. Seeing no other options, I paid him a visit.

He had three main philosophies for treating cancer: 1. Use only treatments which have been tested in clinical trials and been proven to work; 2. Use multiple treatments at once to target cancer's multiple pathways; and 3. Do no harm; or, in other words, don't use any treatments that will make the patient sick. He spent an hour laying out a plan for a course of treatment and repeatedly told me that my cancer wasn't as serious as the other doctors had made it out to be. I walked out of his office able to breathe for the first time in months.

I started on a range of treatments, including some that boosted my immune system and others that kept my metabolism in check. I felt relatively good on these treatments, so aside from taking dozens of pills every day, and going to New York once a month for injections, I was mostly able to get back to my life.

The treatments cost almost as much money as I made in a year, so we had to set about finding a way to raise and earn a lot of extra money. Fortunately, once again, our friends and family came through for us. Through my GiveForward site, fundraisers, and lots of generous donations, we began to collect enough money to cover treatments. I also started an Etsy site and we put our spare room on AirBnB. In addition to treating cancer and keeping up with my day job, I also became a small business owner: anything to afford treatments.

The first scan I had one month after these new treatments started, in April 2015, showed that the cancer was stable. The next scan, three months later, showed that the cancer was actually shrinking.

And then came the scan in November, which showed that the cancer was beginning to spread again, to more lymph nodes. My doctor offered a number of additional, and naturally even more expensive, treatments and we made the investment. Andrew and I even travelled to Germany for a few weeks for some of the most cutting-edge options.

Since then the cancer has continued to spread, slowly but surely, and we have continued to keep fighting. We live, like many advanced cancer patients do, from scan to scan. We watch, with baited breath, to see if the cancer is spreading or growing, and we make new treatment decisions based on the information we are given. I am constantly trying new things, adding new treatments, researching new supplements, testing out new ideas. My home is filled with equipment for treating cancer: a special sauna, a BioMat, infrared lamps... you name it. I now spend several hours every day in one kind of treatment or another. I also have compiled a wonderful, beautiful array of healers. I have an acupuncturist, a Qi Gong teacher, a Reiki master, a therapist, a Rolfer, a chiropractor and many others. These people keep me well, both physically and spiritually, and I know I would not have survived this long without them.

The story of my medical journey continues to unfold. It has been the most challenging experience of my life. I have lost hope, many times. I have wanted to give up, many days. There is a constant battle that goes on inside me to stay positive, to keep going, to keep taking on the tremendous weight of trying to save, or at least extend, my own life, every single day. But I have also learned more, in the last three years, about the true nature of life than I learned in the thirty I lived before that. I have found hundreds of resources in smart friends and wise counsels that have gotten me through. I have uncovered tremendous lessons about how to thrive, how to find meaning and how to love life, even when all of the cards seemed stacked against me. The rest of this book contains those precious, hard-won lessons: how to face down crisis with courage, and live like you mean it.

MIND

Connecting to ourselves, and being a friend to our own minds, is one of the hardest, bravest and most beautiful things we can do. Our relationships with ourselves are the source of the sacred, the healing and the meaning in our lives.

Courage Club Rule #1:

KNOW YOU ARE ENOUGH

"And if I asked you to name all of the things
you loved, how long would it take for you
to name yourself?"

UNKNOWN AUTHOR

Along my journey with cancer, there have been several moments when it's felt like I was standing in quicksand. I couldn't seem to get myself out of emotional trouble, and the more I struggled the further down I sank and the harder it became for anyone else to see, hear or help me.

One of those moments came in the fall of 2015. On this day something seemingly insignificant happened: a friend emailed to say that she had to change our plans in order to squeeze in a visit to see another friend's new baby. It was so minor, so inoffensive, so normal for the excitement of a new baby to take precedent over other, more everyday social engagements. And yet, this small announcement broke something inside of me. It reinforced a message I had been telling myself for months — that I was worthless — and it sent me on a spiral like nothing before.

This idea hadn't come out of nowhere. It had been bred from a lifetime of messages about the importance of becoming a mother. My mother was a midwife, and I grew up surrounded by pregnant women. I helped raise my younger brother and countless cousins and neighbor kids, and by age six I'd mastered diapers, swaddling and heating up bottles. Growing up and as a young adult I was in no rush, but motherhood was often on my mind. I heard a name and thought, "That would make a beautiful name for a girl." I learned something new and thought, "This is something I want to teach my children." I traveled to a new place and imagined bringing my children there someday. Many of my life goals were deeply intertwined with motherhood: I needed to figure out how to eat clean before I had children, how to save money better, how to become more patient, all so I could be a better mother. If my life was a giant compass, motherhood was my north pole.

As responsible young adults, my husband and I had pulled out our calendars, taken a hard look at our careers, our goals, and major life events and penciled in September 2013 as the month we would start trying for a family. Life, as they say, had other plans.

Just months before that date rolled around, the setbacks began to pile up. First, I was diagnosed with Graves' disease and was told that as long as I was on medication I couldn't get pregnant. Most people could successfully get off meds within a year, though. Not a problem. It just meant a temporary delay in our plans.

Then I was diagnosed with cancer. On the day of my diagnosis, I told my medical team that I didn't care about keeping my breasts — I only cared about preserving my fertility. I was immediately put through fertility treatments and successfully froze my embryos. A double mastectomy, of course, meant I wouldn't be able to breastfeed my children, but this was a loss I could manage.

Then, eventually, my cancer metastasized. I was diagnosed with Stage 4 cancer. This was the final blow.

In the months right after my recurrence, I didn't even think about motherhood. All I could think about was doing everything I could to stay alive. But as treatments wore on, and it seemed like I might live longer than had initially been expected, the idea of motherhood crept back into my mind. The problem now was that many of my previously open doors to motherhood were closing. As long as I was on treatments, I couldn't get pregnant — and I had no idea if I would ever be off treatments. As long as I was paying so much for them, there was no chance I would be able to afford a surrogate, let alone a child. Cost aside, with a Stage 4 cancer diagnosis it would make it very difficult to find an adoption agency that would allow me to adopt. And then, of course, there was one more painfully obvious question: what right did I have, as someone with a technically terminal diagnosis, to bring a child into this world?

All of this led me to face down my BIG PAIN, which was: If I but couldn't be a mother, what was the purpose of living?

I could not even *imagine* what my life would be without children. I couldn't understand what would make that life meaningful. I didn't see how I was of any worth to society, to my family and, if I was being honest, to myself. All around me were women raising children. My social media was flooded with birth announcements and photos of new babies. Each time another friend got pregnant, I felt a little more left behind, left out and misunderstood. I couldn't relate to my friends with kids. I couldn't empathize with their challenges. I couldn't fully understand the joys of their celebrations. I was increasingly excluded from the "Mommy Club" and it made me feel increasingly sad. It made my life feel increasingly pointless. It made me, as a person, feel increasingly worthless.

At first, I coped with my grief by digging in my heels. Somehow, I thought, I will survive against all odds, and against all odds I will have children. I clung more tightly than ever to the idea of becoming a mother one day. It felt, almost literally, like my life depended on it. I wrote a blog post making a declaration that no matter what, I was going to be a momma. I had always been an "if you just set your mind to it" kind of gal, and I thought that if I wanted something badly enough, I could get it.

But I am also a planner. I like to pave a clear path forward and the truth was I had no path to achieve this goal. There was a mountain of unknowns and a minefield of obstacles in my way. I thought that clinging to my dreams was the right thing to do, but in reality, it felt like drinking poison. It meant that the purpose and worth of my life relied on something that didn't yet exist, which in turn meant that my life in its current form was fundamentally flawed. It meant that every time I saw someone else achieving my dream, it felt like a punch to the gut. Why didn't *my* dreams get to come true? Why did *they* get to have what *I* wanted? And it meant that every setback in my cancer journey, whether minor or major, felt like falling further down the hill, stumbling farther and farther away from the finish line.

Instead of my resolve rooting me in hope and determination, it had actually rooted me in suffering. And that suffering came to a culmination on the day I got that email in the fall of 2015.

I was at work, and after I read the email, I immediately gathered up my things and headed for the door. I hadn't even reached the elevator before the tears started streaming. I walked to the nearby park, collapsed onto a bench, and fell into uncontrollable sobs. All I could think was that I was not as important to my friends as someone with a baby was; that having a baby makes a life valuable and worthy;

that I would never have that. My life would never have value. I would never have worth.

None of these things were actually true, but at the time my head barely knew that, and my heart most certainly did not. It created a grief so intense that it felt physically painful. I remember calling my husband and telling him I was in bad shape. He attempted to console me, but there was no point. I was in too much pain to be talked down.

I eventually stopped crying and tried to let my mind go blank, tried to let go of all of the pain. I wanted to feel nothing. I wanted to be numb. I eventually stopped responding to Andrew, absentmindedly hung up, and tucked my phone away. I stood up and began to wander the streets of DC in the mid-afternoon. It was an aimless, hopeless wandering, the kind where being hit by a car didn't seem like the worst possible end. Eventually, I wandered into a restaurant and consciously ate the unhealthiest thing I could imagine: broccoli cheddar soup and brownies. I was normally afraid of anything with sugar, of anything that might feed my cancer — but that day I wanted to feed my cancer, wanted to give up and give in to the deadly disease that was ruining my life.

I only vaguely remember the hour-plus drive home. When I arrived, Andrew tried to comfort me, to no avail. I knew my distress wasn't rational — which meant that no rational argument could bring me back. Instead, I just sobbed and clutched at my breaking heart and tried to put into words what it feels like to lose your life's purpose, to believe with all of your being that you have no worth.

At some point, I stumbled to our medicine cabinet and found all of our pain pills. Maybe if I took a few, the pain would go away for a little while. Maybe if I took a few more, they would take me away and someone else would be responsible for all of this pain. Maybe if I took way more than a few, the pain would go away forever.

It was at this point that my husband finally registered in my line of sight. We were both sitting on the kitchen floor. He had his head in his hands and looked up at me. I saw his fear and his desperation. I heard him say that he wasn't sure he could do this anymore. I had a horrifying moment of clarity. I saw that my pursuit of this unattainable goal wasn't just destroying me, but was on the brink of destroying my marriage. I couldn't continue down this path. I couldn't numb the pain. I had to face it. And I couldn't keep ignoring what I *did* have in my life for the sake of the thing that I wanted, but could not have.

I set down the pills and scrambled over to where he was sitting. I begged and pleaded with him not to give up on me. I didn't realize it at the time, but in that moment I had already begun calling on my own self-advocate. Through the layers and layers of pain and self-loathing, a still, small voice rose up that said: you're worth it.

I tried to compose myself. I knew I could find a way to heal. I reminded myself of all of my previous emotional meltdowns, and how it had always come down to me taking the first step in order to find healing. I would have to be calm in the quicksand, in order to find my eventual freedom from it.

Sitting there on the kitchen floor, I told Andrew I knew I could fix this. When he didn't believe me, I jumped up and grabbed a piece of paper and a pen and quickly scrawled out twelve promises: twelve things I would do to begin to turn my life around, so he wouldn't have to see me go through this kind of pain anymore. He also took his own paper and scrawled out his own promises. Together, we would build a better life we decided.

In many ways, those twelve promises were a foundation for the ten main chapters of this book. They were twelve things I needed to do to reconnect to myself, to come back to my life. I had been so focused on what was lacking in my life, so caught up in grieving what I couldn't have, that I was missing an opportunity to live. Even though I included things on the list like promising to connect more with my husband, cook meals together, do the dishes more, some wise part of my heart knew that the first step must be a reconnection with myself. I needed to find a way to feel worthy again: of my own love, of my husband's love, and of a meaningful life. We cannot have a meaningful life if we do not feel that we deserve it.

The first step was to forgive myself for my breakdown. It is so easy, when we are neck deep in quicksand, to blame ourselves for stepping into it in the first place. But the truth is that I had suffered great losses, earth-shattering losses, and the grief I felt was not out of proportion to what had been taken from me. I had been through multiple traumas in the past few years, and our brains have a tendency to try to protect ourselves from trauma in complicated and sometimes not-such-healing ways. I knew that beating myself up would only force me deeper down. I needed gentleness. I needed kindness. I needed to love myself, even in my most unlovable moment...*especially* in my most unlovable moment.

So I forgave myself. I forgave myself publicly, in fact. The next day I posted this on Facebook:

> Perhaps it's the spirit of Yom Kippur in the air, perhaps it's the difficulty that the last few days have presented, perhaps it's just the right time, but I want to ask for forgiveness. And I find it necessary to begin with myself... The chilly weather reminds me of all that I've lost, all that I can no longer have in this life, all the suffering that a lifetime is capable of holding and makes me question the incredible emotional and financial lengths I go to every day to try to remain on the earth a little longer. But I forgive myself and my brain for this trick that it plays on me. I forgive the human tendencies of trauma to hijack our hope, to carve out an emptiness and fill it with helplessness. It is not me, it is not my power, it is not my resilience that fills me with these dark thoughts, it is my trauma. I forgive the feelings of worthlessness and shame and pain. They don't know any better. They only know what they've had to endure and are activating a primal part of me that just wants protection...I forgive myself for these missteps, for falling down when I generally work so hard to keep trudging onward. I hope all

of you who have had to experience trauma in your lives can do the same. Sending love and light and all the hope I can muster.

Even though I'd already shared many private parts of my journey on my blog, forgiving myself publicly felt like a radical act. Society had ingrained in me that we are supposed to be self-effacing, not self-forgiving. Aren't we supposed to silently beat ourselves up and hope no one else noticed that we messed up? I'd been doing those things all my life, and they'd mostly gotten me through my pre-cancer world. But now, with all the grief and fear and anger and trauma piled up on my doorstep, I had to do something braver than before. A public apology kept me accountable and made forgiveness feel like the act of strength and bravery that it was.

I then turned to all of my favorite meditation books and sought out self-Metta meditations, also known as loving kindness meditations. I still hadn't convinced myself that I deserved my own love, but I thought I could at least take a first step with the intention of self-love. For me, mantras have always been a wonderful way to practice concentration and create a deep inner peace.

So I began with a self-love mantra. For several nights in a row, I silently repeated to myself: "I love you. I forgive you." It was such a foreign feeling to send these messages to myself. I realized I hadn't ever taken the time to tell myself that before: "I love you. I forgive you." My brain felt much more comfortable sitting in judgment of my many faults, berating me for my many mistakes. But saying those six small words allowed me to relax into myself. I could let go of the self-criticisms that took up so much of my time and energy. I could let go of the negative toxic thoughts about myself I often held onto all day long. We often hear about how toxic it can be to hold onto resentment toward others, but rarely do we think about the resentment that we hold against ourselves. It felt wonderful to let those go, for at least 30 peaceful minutes, before bed each night.

Once I had begun making these self-love mantras a daily practice, I was ready to tackle the messiest piece of the puzzle. I needed to let go of the idea of being a mother. For so long, I'd thought that the source of my grief had been my inability to be a mother. What I discovered, however, was that the true source of my grief was actually the feeling that *not* being a mother made me worthless. So I developed my own simple mantra: "I am worthy, even if I cannot be a mother." I will say that I did not like this mantra. I did not believe it. It sounded like wishy-washy fantasy. I had a list miles-long of reasons it was wrong. But I knew it needed to be said.

I began repeating it silently to myself. I knew immediately that I'd hit a trigger, because tears started to well up, and quickly began to flow. Before I knew it, I was sobbing. Somehow that one simple sentence was breaking something in my mind wide open. I still didn't believe it was true, but I kept saying it.

This went on for several nights. I would lie down, find my breath, and begin repeating the sentence: "I am worthy, even if I cannot be a mother." The tears would roll until I stopped. Eventually, I could say the words to myself without crying, but I still wasn't sure I believed them.

By this time, the holidays were rolling around and we started to get holiday cards in the mail. I took a few minutes one day to collect all the cards with family photos and hang them up on our fridge. Most of the families staring back at me were my friends with their new babies or toddlers: so many beautiful, smiling, happy families. So many reminders of the life I had so desperately yearned for, but could not have. I waited for the familiar pang in my heart, waited for the grief to roll in, for the jealousy to sting, and the anger to burn. But it didn't come. Instead, I heard my mind say, "The life in these photos isn't for me right now."

It was in that moment that I realized that my identity had shifted. Instead of this idea of myself as a mother, I had become something else in my own mind. I had become who I actually was. And instead of seeing this childless woman as less than, as lacking, I finally realized that I saw her for what she really was: powerful and resilient, interesting and interested, and above all, worthy. I loved her, and I loved her life. It felt a bit like magic or witchcraft. All I had done was practice some self-compassion and self-forgiveness, set an intention, and said a few simple words to myself that I didn't even believe — and it had led to a powerful inner shift.

I still feel sad about not being a mother. The progress I have made doesn't mean the grief is gone. Mother's Day is particularly difficult. I still have moments when I wistfully wish I were spending hours a day nursing and burping or reading and playing, and not treating my own cancer. But I have never stopped appreciating this life that I do have. When I am being harsh with myself I try to remember to be kinder. And when I need a break, from the world and my own self-criticisms, I can always go back to my mantras.

I believe the cards are often stacked against us when it comes to our own self-worth. We live in a world of scarcity. Nothing is ever enough. We aren't pretty enough, strong enough, or smart enough. We haven't spent enough time, tried hard enough or achieved enough. I believe that the only antidote to scarcity is enoughness. We are all enough. And the one place where there is never scarcity is in our ability to love. Love is abundant. We all need to realize that the person most deserving of our love is the one staring back at us in the mirror. No matter what you have been through, no matter what you have done, no matter how you feel, you are enough. You are worthy. We all are.

Courage Club Rule #2:

ACCEPT EVERYTHING ABOUT YOURSELF

"Accept everything about yourself — I mean everything. You are you and that is the beginning and the end — no apologies, no regrets."

HENRY KISSINGER

I was once the reigning queen of Not Accepting Things.

One of my greatest skill sets in this arena was writing angry letters. This was before we boiled our complaints down to 140-character rants on Twitter, or single star reviews on Yelp. If I found a company's product or service to be lacking, I would write a strongly worded letter and send it off via good old USPS. I was particularly focused on incidents that felt unjust: if myself or another customer were treated unfairly, or a promotion or product was not as advertised, I would make sure that company knew how I felt. I tried not to be petty and often felt that I was standing up for the little guy, that I was righting wrongs. On occasion, though, I did get a bit carried away. (True story: I once wrote to a cheese company telling them their cheese wasn't melting properly. I ended up with more free cheese than I care to discuss and a free sample every time they invented a new style. Apparently, I got myself on their "people with strong opinions about cheese" list.)

I also put my written rage to other, arguably more productive, uses, and would write letters to Congress about laws and policies I cared about. In high school I wrote a letter to the principal of a rival basketball team, because I felt the derogatory remarks their fans had made about my team were inappropriate at best, and racially charged at worst. I successfully got pep rallies banned at that school for the remainder of the year — and made life-long enemies of hundreds of young men. It was awesome.

I took some amount of pride in not accepting the world's injustices (or mediocre cheeses). But the truth is that my inability to accept went beyond standing up for what was right. I aimed those same judgments at myself. I have always been a perfectionist — and have, naturally, perfected my ability to tear myself down. If I ever did anything that upset someone else or made me look inadequate, a rigid inner monologue would ruthlessly take over. I'd ruminate on what I had done wrong until I felt sufficiently bullied into not making the same mistake again. I also had a hard time accepting my emotional responses. I considered myself too emotional, over reactive, too sensitive. Instead of being kind and gentle to myself, trying to soothe whatever ached when I was sad or angry or afraid, I would belittle myself for not having more emotional control. My mind was convinced that loving myself, accepting myself, and giving myself a break, were not ways to succeed in life.

I had rarely felt a sense of acceptance for my own life, particularly my life *right now*. It's not that I didn't enjoy my life; I simply had a pretty bad case of the "grass is always greener" syndrome. Wherever I was, the next place was definitely going to be better. When I was in college I knew all of my problems would be solved when I graduated and got a job. After my first challenging job I knew a career switch would help things improve. When I lived in one city, I just *knew* my life would be so much easier if I lived somewhere else. In some ways I suppose it was a form of sad optimism, always believing my life was going to improve; but in many ways, it just meant that I rarely appreciated what I had when I had it.

My life crisis of being diagnosed with cancer rearranged, confused and complicated this system of non-acceptance. You might expect that being diagnosed with cancer at the age of 30 would have riled up that inner, rage-filled letter writer. In many ways, it was the greatest injustice of my life, far more unfair and life altering than any of the offenses I had previously encountered.

And yet, the overwhelming feeling the day I was diagnosed was a relief. Upon hearing the nurse say the words, "I'm sorry to tell you that it's breast cancer," I felt tears well up in my eyes — and then a huge sigh of relief escaped my lips. It seemed bizarre, even in the moment, but I think I was just relieved to have an answer. I'd spent two weeks worried sick about the lump I had found in my breast, and I'd been waiting five grueling days for the biopsy results. To know what was going on meant a plan could be put into place, which meant I could stop wondering, and start doing. It was relieving not to have to worry and wonder, and to instead be able to start moving forward with all that had to be done.

After my diagnosis, I was forced in rapid succession to accept a great number of things: I had to be on chemo for five months. I would lose all my hair. I had to have fertility treatments if I ever wanted to have a child. I would have to cut back on my work schedule. I wouldn't be able to travel for a while. I would probably have to undergo a double mastectomy.

In some ways, accepting the *idea* of all of these things was easy. I was in crisis mode, and this is what had to be done. In crisis mode, you just keep saying "yes." You just keep putting one foot in front of the other. You don't have time to deal with whether or not it's fair, how it ruins your plans, or what complex emotional response you would have if you had more time to process it. This can be a productive way to respond in times of crisis, but this kind of acceptance is shallow and perfunctory, and often leads to what I call "delayed-onset grief."

For example, I knew I would lose all of my hair, and had "accepted" that this would happen. I went onto Etsy and purchased both a colorful assortment of head wraps, to match any outfit, and a plethora of dangly earrings to compliment said head wraps. I pulled my long hair back into a tight bun and put one of the head wraps on. I thought I pulled it off pretty well. I snapped a picture and texted my best friend. "I can totally do this!" I wrote.

But ultimately, letting go of my hair, an enormous piece of my physical identity, was not so easy. I nervously made an appointment to have my hair stylist cut it short as an emotional stepping-stone to losing it all. I felt naked as I left the salon that day, having gone from hair that fell halfway down my back, to a pixie cut. It was only a few more days before my hair started to come out at a rapid pace. I knew the moment to shave it all was growing near, but I was terrified. I was so distressed about the prospect that I slept on the couch one night, not wanting to keep my husband up as I tossed and turned. At around five in the morning, I finally gave up on sleep and made the decision that I would shave my head that day. I couldn't take the anxiety anymore. I let myself cry for about an hour, mourning the loss of my hair and marking my transition into becoming someone who looked like a cancer patient.

Despite the many #baldisbeautiful selfies I posted, and the months that I spent sans head wrap just letting myself be a bald woman in the world, I never really accepted the loss of my hair. I hated what I saw in the mirror and felt desperate, every day, for my hair to grow back and look "normal" again.

In fact, all that acceptance work I thought I had done early on after my diagnosis, turned out to be a coping mechanism hiding an iceberg's worth of rejection just below the surface. I had been in crisis mode doing what I had to do in the moment. It's an excellent way to prevent ourselves from becoming overwhelmed when crisis hits, but it doesn't mean we won't suffer the emotional consequences later. I eventually grew deeply bitter about many of the things I'd thought I'd "accepted," in part, I think, because I felt like I was forced into letting them enter my life. By the time I was finished with all of my treatments, I was aware of a deep thread of anger, bitterness, and resentment running through my life. My rage-filled letter writer was back. If only there had been someone to blame for my cancer, that person definitely would have received several strongly worded letters.

I was still working to overcome my anger and bitterness about cancer when a recurrence came walking into my life. Unlike the last diagnosis, this one came with a bunch of stuff I just could not accept. My cancer was now Stage 4. Stage 4 is incurable and terminal. I would have cancer forever. Even though it was just in one small lymph node, it would quickly spread to my organs. It was chemo-resistant, radiation-resistant, and inoperable. There were no good treatments left for me. This cancer would kill me unless something else did first. The odds were against surviving much longer than a year.

Death. There is nothing in the world that we are more trained to resist. Our will to live is programmed into our DNA. Our avoidance of all things related to death is deeply ingrained in Western culture, much to the harm of the dying. If you have had any experience facing down your own mortality, you understand how deep the resistance runs. Our entire being has a tendency to tighten and recoil at the mere suggestion that we contemplate death.

It was around then that I began the great balancing act of acceptance that I continue to this day. On one hand, I couldn't accept that there were no treatment options available to me. I didn't want to accept the fact that my cancer would spread fast and kill me quickly. This *lack* of acceptance enabled me to find doctors and healers and a myriad of experts who saw cancer differently, who believed that there are plenty of non-traditional and alternative treatment options out there that could, at the very least, slow my cancer down.

On the other hand, I had to find ways to accept; not only that I might have this cancer for the rest of my life, but that this cancer might kill me. Fully accepting our own deaths is not a light practice. I spent the first year after my recurrence convinced that I would find some kind of miracle cure, that eventually the cancer would go away and I would be able to live my life again. But that didn't happen. Over the course of three scans that first year, the cancer first stabilized, then shrank and then began to spread again.

When I learned that the cancer had spread, it crushed my remaining hopes about someday being cancer-free, about someday living a "normal life." Yet I still didn't want to accept that death might be waiting for me, just around the corner. At first the thought of my impending death sunk me into a deep depression. I was crushed under the weight of this great unknown, this terrifying potential reality. My greatest fear, this abstract concept of my own death, followed me around like a vulture, constantly circling through the big and little moments of my days. While planning an event at work, I'd wonder if I would be well enough to attend. A song would come on, and I'd wonder if it would make my friends cry when they heard it after I was gone, or if they would play it at my funeral. I was constantly thinking about my own death and those thoughts often sent me into a panic.

It quickly became unbearable so I did the only thing I could think of doing: I began working toward the acceptance of both my life and my death. The first step was to deconstruct my resistance. Death was this massive, abstract concept, so I had to break it down. What about death was so scary? I thought about becoming extremely ill and being in a lot of pain. I thought about getting stuck spending all of my time in hospitals and with doctors again. I thought about endless surgeries and procedures to try and extend my life just a little longer. I thought about having to say good-bye to my friends and family. I thought about being forced to see everyone I know go through the pain of losing me. And more painful than any of these, I thought about losing my husband, leaving him to live the rest of his life without me, not being able to be there for him when he would need someone the most.

The next step was to determine what I had control over. At least half of my fears were rooted in losing control. Death felt deeply disempowering, like a slow and steady loss of all control. The other half of my fears came from the pain my friends and family would go through. I had little control over that — but at least making my death easier on me, might make it easier on them.

I decided that I would have an empowered death. Many people write a birth plan; I would have a death plan, reflective of what I value most. As much as I could, I would make decisions about the end of my life that favored dignity. I would find ways to live my last days where *I* wanted to be, not caught up in the throes of Western medicine. I would bring in healers and experts, people with experience in facing death, and I would surround myself and my friends and family with their wisdom and comfort.

In the process of trying to accept my greatest fear, breaking it down into smaller pieces made it more manageable, more tangible. Determining what I had control over allowed me to take the sting out of some of the fear. I had to put some amount of trust in myself and in the universe. I'm not ready to face death today, but I know in my bones that I will get there. My family and friends will find a way to bear the weight of whatever ends up happening to me and I will find the right healers and experts to help guide us when the time comes.

This rumble with accepting death is a constant one. It's hard to know when I should keep my attention squarely on living and surviving, and when it's helpful to turn my attention to death. I once read a story about the people of Bhutan, a country that continually ranks as the happiest in all of Asia. The author claimed that the people of Bhutan are so happy because they have a culture of contemplating death every day. I don't think contemplating death necessarily makes me happy; if I let it go too far, it can make me feel defeated in my journey. But I do think that living so close to death, and allowing the idea of death in, has helped me to live a fuller life.

I no longer suffer from the "grass is always greener" syndrome. The grass could very well be as green as it's ever going to get, right now. And right now isn't always perfect. It isn't even always pleasant. I spend hours every day focused on cancer. I'm either undergoing some kind of treatment, or organizing my pills, or visiting a doctor, or making a healthy meal. Cancer means my life doesn't include many of the things I wish it did: children, the chance to really focus on my career, the opportunity to travel as much as I once did. Every three months I'm faced with scans, which I once described as the equivalent of waiting for a college acceptance letter every three months, except you only applied to one school and if you don't get in your life literally ends.

I essentially have two choices. I can feel sorry for myself and bitter and angry about my life. Or I can do something I have never been able to do before, and accept my life as it is: warts, cancer and all. Thinking about death, knowing how close it may be, gives me an incredibly strong argument for the latter approach.

This is not the life I thought I would lead, and it's a life filled with hardship — but it is also a life filled with incredible opportunities. When you live your life so close to something so challenging, it creates a space for you to engage only with what is real, to focus only on what matters most, and to interact with others from a space of deep intention. Being part of the cancer community, being able to focus so much of my time and attention on healing, health, wellness, nutrition, and spirituality is not a terrible way to live.

So while I have come closer to accepting death, I have also wholeheartedly accepted my life. The last step is to accept myself, particularly my emotions. This one is a daily struggle. I remember exploding in the kitchen one morning, feeling overwhelmed with fear, cursing myself for not being able to move beyond whatever had been nagging at me. My husband looked at me and said, "Katie, the first thing you need to do is just accept that you feel the way you feel."

I took a deep breath and realized that the thing I was feeling so bad and scared about, was completely worthy of acceptance. Of course, I felt afraid. It made perfect sense given my situation. Somehow, this recognition made me immediately feel better. It was as if my emotions were screaming children who just wanted acknowledgment. Once I gave them the attention they wanted, instead of trying to ignore them, they immediately stopped screaming.

Accepting our emotions is an exercise in self-compassion and self-care. It's easy to berate ourselves for our reactions, to want to push difficult emotions out of our minds, to avoid confronting the fear or anger or grief that swims around just below the surface. But acknowledging and accepting those difficult emotions is a beautiful act of self-care. "I see you, Fear. I accept that you're here. I get it." It's easy to say, but difficult to do; yet, the end result can be transformational.

Cancer has put me to the ultimate test. I have learned what the first steps of tough, deep, painful acceptance feel like. I have had to deconstruct my resistance and figure out what I can control in order to face down those big scary fears. I have had to let go of my "grass is always greener" days and come to love and accept the life that I am living today because I do not have tomorrow promised to me. And I have taken the first steps in learning how to accept myself and my emotions. There are a thousand opportunities every day to beat ourselves up and berate ourselves for failing to meet our own high standards, but that means that there are also a thousand opportunities to take a deep breath, show ourselves a little compassion, and send our hearts some acceptance.

Courage Club Rule #3:

BE VULNERABLE

"Vulnerability sounds like truth and feels like courage. Truth and courage aren't always comfortable, but they are never weakness."

BRENÉ BROWN

For much of my life, I would describe my relationship with vulnerability as *allergic*. I wanted nothing to do with vulnerability. I wrote it off as a weakness and deeply loathed it anytime it entered my periphery. I held my insecurities in and performed invincible and confident so well that I often fooled everyone around me. The more insecure I was on the inside, the more confident I made myself appear on the outside. I didn't notice it during high school, but years later when I looked back on my senior yearbook, I found that nearly half of the comments about me were something along the lines of, "You always really intimidated me but once I got to know you I realized you were really nice and down to earth." My dorm freshmen year of college was a hallway of freshman with just four seniors in suites at the end. I quickly discovered that nearly half the residents assumed I was one of the seniors. It couldn't have been my looks, because I've always looked young for my age. No, I believe the mix-up was the result of the iron vest of confidence I wore to cover up a deep well of anxiety and insecurity. Being intimidating felt better than being hurt.

I was deeply convinced that if I showed anyone who I really was that I wouldn't be loved or even liked. I always had many acquaintances but very few close friends. It felt exhausting to let people in, to take off the armor I had so diligently constructed and worn for so long.

Of course, it was equally exhausting to put on a performance of confidence, to try and play perfect all the time. I was the girl who would decide to bake cupcakes for work, spend all night baking said cupcakes, ruin the first batch, have a meltdown, run to the store, buy more ingredients, make a second batch, go to bed late, wake up early the next morning, bring my cupcakes into work — and when someone thanked me, say, "Oh, it was nothing!" Perhaps I confided in a few friends about my epic cupcake meltdown — but generally I wanted to be seen as having my shit superbly together. I had perfected the *performance* of perfect, but inside I was anything but.

When I was diagnosed with Graves' disease, I was beyond embarrassed at the sudden decline in my health. I felt like I had somehow instigated my own illness, and I was mortified by my symptoms, which left me feeling out of shape and lazy. I told very few people about what was going on. There was no public Facebook post, no blog post, no coming out. I just silently suffered on my own: locked inside for nearly a month, eating endless bowls of Honey Nut Cheerios and watching every single episode of Star Trek Voyager (I know it's not the most critically acclaimed in the series but I love me some lady starship captains and hot female borgs!)

When I was diagnosed with cancer I felt quite different. On one hand it felt big, important and life changing from the start. On the other hand, having cancer shielded me from the scary possibility of criticism and judgment. You can't really pick on or judge the experience of someone with cancer. People do, of course, but being able to play "the cancer card" on anyone trying to attack me made being open a little easier. Having cancer made my public space a little bit safer.

So I began by posting blogs about how I was feeling from one day to the next. My posts began on the lighthearted side. I took the opportunity to laugh at my situation when I could. I wrote an ode to my hair before I shaved it all off, in which I apologized for a lengthy list of offenses, including the perms I got in the '80s, the two decades I spent obsessing over my bangs, and the sometimes excessive amount of hairspray that was involved in both endeavors. But as my journey with cancer got bumpier and more complicated, I started to let that stuff out as well. I wrote about how afraid I felt when it looked like treatments weren't working. I spilled my anger and grief over coming to terms with losing my breasts. I tried to explain the desperate pain I felt over having my dreams of motherhood taken away from me.

Often when I revealed such deep and difficult emotions in a blog post, I would walk away from the computer with an immediate vulnerability hangover. For me, vulnerability hangovers are ripe with self-doubt and a sense of insecurity: "Did I say too much? What will people think of me? I shouldn't have gone so far." In the depths of such a hangover, it's easy to brood on all the things I could be judged for, all the reasons I shouldn't have shared so much.

Often, however, I would find that my worries were needless. The responses I received were almost always incredibly supportive. The more I shared and the deeper I went, the stronger the responses were. It made me realize that my suffering was just a reflection of the suffering that we all face at some point in our lives. The more open I was, the more people could relate to me and the more connected they could feel. Being vulnerable in writing, through a blog, still allows some degree of protection, but I had found a space where I could say exactly how I felt, where I could truly reveal myself and all of my messy emotions. It felt like practice for real world vulnerability, a skill that couldn't have come at a better moment.

Before cancer, I was fiercely independent. I stayed above the fray of vulnerability by refusing to rely on anybody... ever. I was the baby stealing the spoon away from my mom because I was pretty dang sure I could handle this feeding thing myself. Yet, having cancer meant I needed help, a lot of help. If it hadn't been for my incredible support network, making me meals a few times a week and bringing me groceries while I was on chemo, I think either my husband would have collapsed from exhaustion or we would have gone hungry. Learning to accept this kind of help was hard. I always preferred to be the giver in relationships, consistent with the pulled together performance I was always putting on.

But I also needed another kind of help. I needed more emotional support than I ever had before. And to get that support I needed to be vulnerable.

At some points, this form of vulnerability was manageable: my life was so overwhelming, I had no time or energy to pretend to be pulled together. But even this forced vulnerability wasn't always easy for me. Once, after a procedure early in my treatment, which left me in excruciating pain, I'd been taking painkillers and keeping a steady stream of ice packs going, but I was afraid of the pain becoming unbearable. My husband needed to teach a class that evening but I was afraid to be left alone. We reached out to our support group and asked if anyone could come and just sit with me. Within a few minutes we had a schedule of people lined up. Being sad, scared, and in pain in front of my friends was not initially comfortable for me, but I knew I needed company, distraction, and support in that moment — more than I needed to protect myself from being vulnerable. So they came, and they sat, and I got through the night because of their goodwill and my willingness to acknowledge that I needed them.

Another time, later in the year, I had a rather embarrassing episode, which I later chalked up to PTSD (Post-traumatic stress disorder), or "trauma brain." I was finally starting to feel better after my last round of chemo and I was thrilled to be able to run a few light errands. I got myself ready and put on real clothes and makeup for the first time in over a week. I was still too weak to walk far or take the Metro, but I figured I could drive. I got all my stuff together and was so excited to be leaving the house for the first time since chemo over a week ago.

But when I tried to open my car, it wouldn't unlock. My key fob had run out of batteries. I knew my fob had a backup key inside, so I tried to use that, but still the lock wouldn't turn. It was a frustrating thing, to be sure, but in that moment I reacted in a way completely out of proportion with the circumstances. I started screaming and yelling at the car. I stomped inside and felt myself become completely overwhelmed by anger and rage.

After a week of fighting to feel better, preceded by five months of the same, I just could not take one more letdown. Cancer forces you to battle against feelings of helplessness and a total lack of control, and this one small thing, not being able to get into my car, just destroyed me. I screamed and slammed my hands against the table over and over until I was fairly certain they might be bruised. I threw pillows. I yelled. I cried. I collapsed on the floor. It was a temper tantrum, the likes of which I hadn't thrown since I was a child. I've always been a bit explosive when it comes to my emotions, and my inability to keep a lid on them or brush stuff off has been a source of deep shame — but this was on a whole new level.

Once I had calmed down, I realized that despite the shame and confusion this recent episode had caused, I needed help. I decided to phone a friend who I knew also struggled with anger issues. I started the call with: "So about anger...."

We ended up talking for a long time, discussing my recent outbursts and how uncontrollable they felt. We talked about the darkness that felt like it had overtaken my life, the feeling that the universe was no longer on my side. He didn't have cancer but could definitely relate. The universe was out to get us both, we agreed. We talked about trauma, a topic in which he had long been interested, and together we found resources in the forms of books I could read and specialists in the area that I could see. Ultimately, this friend ended up being a critical part of my survival. Because I'd been willing to step outside of my normal safe space and lay down my burdens for someone else to carry, I received the emotional support I needed through one of the darkest times in my life. It took a lot to let down my guard, put away my armor, show up messy and unkempt, and let myself be seen in my darkest hour.

Ultimately, what we all need in life, whether we have cancer or not, is for someone else to say, "I see you." But we can't be seen unless we are willing to show the world who we really are.

I've found that vulnerability takes practice. Yet, there is a familiar ebb and flow to the process. It begins with revealing something we might not normally share. Sometimes this is a purposeful decision, like my decision to reach out to friends when I needed support. Sometimes this happens by accident when something unexpected happens that forces us to drop our guard — like the time I sobbed through the hallways of my office when my oncologist called me at work to tell me the cancer was back.

Following the reveal is often the vulnerability hangover: a period of painful self-doubt in which we wonder what on earth we were thinking. Anytime you put a piece of yourself out into the world, whether it's sharing something intimate with a friend or putting your art or your work on display, it's easy to be overcome by the vulnerability hangover. If we allow our shame and sense of self-doubt to take over, this part can be so painful that it will make us never want to be vulnerable again. I have found that it's critical to embrace this hangover with the same kind of gentle care we might a real hangover. For a real hangover, we might lay off the alcohol for a little while, rest as much as we can, and drink as much water as possible. For a vulnerability

Sell your books at sellbackyourBook.com!

Go to sellbackyourBook.com and get an instant price quote. We even pay the shipping - see what your old books are worth today!

Inspected By:Maria_Gonzalez

00027701031

1031   G

hangover, sometimes it's necessary to back away from being so vulnerable for a while — just to give our hearts a break, allow time and space for those feelings of self-doubt, and feed our hearts as much self-love as we can. The great thing about a vulnerability hangover, just like a real one, is that it eventually does go away.

The good news, of course, is that more often than not, the next step in the vulnerability process is connection. By being willing to share (particularly the most difficult, most embarrassing, most shameful parts of ourselves, but also our hopes, our dreams, and our deepest truths) we allow others to really see us. By doing so we allow their humanity to connect to our humanity. I have found that the number of people who can relate to different parts of my journey is not at all limited to those who have had cancer. Suffering is suffering, and the feelings of grief, anger, sadness and fear are often the same across a multitude of afflictions and situations.

The work I've done on my own vulnerability has transformed many areas of my life and created much deeper and more meaningful connections, even within the relationships that were already close. For example, previously, instead of being vulnerable and open with my husband about something that was bothering me I would more often than not put on a tough face. This "tough face" meant to protect the emotions seething just below the surface often had the unintended effect of making me appear distracted or short-tempered. Now I try to let my guard down more often. I'll say, "I know I seem grumpy, but I'm really just anxious about this new treatment," or, "I'm sorry I snapped, I'm just feeling really sad about my friend who recently got bad news about her cancer."

Sometimes it's not even easy to recognize why I'm in a funk, let alone explain it to someone else. But three things happen when I can be vulnerable about what is really going on for me. First, it prevents my husband from making the kind of assumptions that we all too often make about each other, such as: "She's upset that I didn't do the dishes/come home on time/clean up my clothes, which is why she's being so short with me right now." In this way, our own insecurities breed insecurities in those around us. Vulnerability can short-circuit this brutal cycle. Second, it allows my husband to meet me where I am and support me through whatever I am going through. In some ways, just explaining how I feel is asking for help, even if that help is simply understanding. And finally, vulnerability breeds those connections. We become closer when we can share, understand, and support.

Ultimately, I have never regretted embracing my vulnerability. I used to believe that my insecurities were what made me unlovable. In reality, the things that make *me* feel insecure are the same things that make us all feel insecure, and if we share those things it makes us so much easier to love. This journey with vulnerability is not without its own pain, but for those courageous enough to practice vulnerable living, the rewards are no less than the love, understanding, and connection we have always sought.

Courage Club Rule #4:

BE HERE, NOW

"To begin to meditate is to look into our lives
with interest in kindness and discover how
to be wakeful and free."

JACK KORNFIELD

Meditation has become one of those things, like drinking green juice, which we all know we *should* be doing, but find to be easier said than done. Ultimately, our world and our brains are wired for distraction. It is rare that our first instinct is for quiet and stillness. Some of us have had amazing experiences with meditation. We have taken a class, gone on a retreat, or just practiced from the comfort of our own home, and had experiences of deep peace or incredible connection. And many more of us likely still haven't figured out what all the hype is about, or have tried meditation only to feel like we are "doing it wrong."

Meditation was something that I struggled to make my own. Over the decade-plus that we've been together, my husband has gone through many periods of intensive meditation. He would practice for hours in a day, go on retreats, and read countless books; he has studied mindfulness and meditation as part of his dissertation. For me, this meant that meditation always felt like *his* thing, and his approach to meditation didn't always feel like it was a good fit for me. I knew it was a tool I could turn to, but it wasn't until I had no other place to turn that I finally learned how meditation and, more specifically, mindfulness, could be my salvation.

Researchers have just recently begun to appreciate the trauma that cancer and cancer treatments can cause for patients. PTSD is finally being diagnosed in cancer patients, although the literature still rarely includes illnesses as a cause of PTSD. But the definition could not be more fitting. PTSD is defined as reaction to a traumatic experience or event that makes a person feel that their life, or the life of a loved one, is threatened. From my own experience, cancer has made me feel that my life is constantly under attack. Even before I was diagnosed Stage 4, I felt terrified for my life throughout and following most of my treatments. In addition, I believe that the physical threat of things like chemotherapy and surgery can be deeply traumatic. The body wants to protect itself and nothing makes it feel less protected than getting poisoned over and over again. I never felt so much like I was dying as when I was on chemotherapy.

During my worst period of PTSD, towards the end of my first 16 rounds of chemo and around the time of my double mastectomy, I had reached a point at which I felt like my normal brain and thought functions had completely stopped working. One of the main symptoms of PTSD is a high state of arousal. For me, this was something akin to living constantly in that moment of a horror movie right before the killer jumps out. I was intensely on edge, from the moment I woke up to the moment I tried to sleep. I was emotional, prone to angry outbursts, easily panicked. I was always agitated and it was literally driving me insane.

Once I suspected I might be suffering from PTSD I began to read books about trauma. Although none of them mentioned illness as a possible cause, they did list all of my symptoms. Reading through the list felt as if someone were secretly recording a day in my life. Now knowing that the symptoms I was experiencing were definitely the result of PTSD, I took the first steps to finding a trauma specialist. A friend suggested I try to find an expert in somatic experiencing and so I set up an appointment with someone in D.C.

The idea behind somatic experiencing came from Dr. Peter Levine. He discovered that even though humans and animals have very similar body- and brain-based survival mechanisms, animals don't suffer from the same kind of PTSD symptoms that humans do. In both humans and animals, it's the Autonomic Nervous System (ANS) that takes over when a life-threatening event occurs. This is also known as our fight, flight, or freeze response. In his research, Dr. Levine discovered that when the ANS was stimulated in animals, their bodies were flooded with energy, as are ours, but they often undertook some kind of behavior to discharge the buildup of energy, such as shaking, heavy breathing, or some other physical response. The problem with humans is our brains. Instead of standing around shaking or running in circles, we will try to rationalize, shame, or judge ourselves out of a situation. This means that the agitation to our systems never gets discharged. It continues to live on in the body in the form of distress of the digestive, immune system, cardiac and respiratory systems, in addition to the psychological symptoms of trauma and PTSD. Somatic experiencing allows the patient to gently bring up and release these energetic traumas that live within the body, allowing our systems to reset and move on from the traumatic event.

For me, this meant becoming deeply mindful of my body and how it related to what was happening in my mind. I would sit across from my therapist and pay very close attention to what I was feeling and how that emotion corresponded to sensations in my body. I carried some emotions like a one-ton weight on my chest, some in my throat where they felt like they were strangling me, and others lived like a pit in my stomach. Working together, we would create gentle flows and movement of some of this trapped energy, allowing it to move through and eventually out of my body. The therapy also allowed me to think about new ways to release any new energy that might get trapped: like going for a run or riding my bike up a hill. This kind of physical movement became critical for my mental well-being.

After just a few sessions I began to feel much more like myself. The agitation slowly dissipated, along with the emotional outbursts and thought spirals that had so trapped me. I hadn't started a regular meditation practice, but I had started a practice of mindfulness. Getting in touch with the connection between my mind and body had opened up a new portal into understanding myself and my experience. We often think of emotions as living in the brain but in reality, we almost always experience them in the body. I think it's why our ancestors believed that emotions came from our heart because we hold on to a great many things in our chest.

Recognizing this connection gave me a new coping mechanism for dealing with overwhelming emotions. Previously, my response had been to ruminate, analyze, judge (and sometimes punish,) and generally, over think whatever I was feeling. If I didn't do this, then I would desperately try to distract myself from my emotion. In my case, this often meant turning to television or obsessive social media engagement. For others, this need for distraction and avoidance can manifest as something as benign as video games or something as dangerous as addiction. My husband had always encouraged me to sit with difficult emotions, but it felt impossible to sit with serious fear without thinking myself into even greater fear. Somehow, sitting with the *physical* feeling of fear was much easier. I could take my thinking brain out of the equation and just allow myself to sit with what fear *feels* like. I could sit with the tightness in my chest, focus on whether it moved or changed, and accept its presence.

What I found was that focusing my attention on the physical feeling almost always made the emotion slowly dissipate. I didn't have to go off and meditate on my own in a dark room for this to work. I could do it anywhere, at any time. It became a wonderful tool for managing the hurdles that cancer threw at me.

Of course, there eventually came a time when cancer again threw me a curveball that set me back into trauma brain. After I was diagnosed with a recurrence that made my cancer incurable and terminal, I was emotionally overwhelmed on a daily basis. I couldn't sleep, couldn't eat, couldn't think straight. Whenever I was alone, even in public, I often found myself in tears. I would look at the living people all around me and the tears would flow for all the life that I felt was being taken away from me. How I longed to have their lives and their problems.

One weekend, Andrew and I accepted a kind offer from our friends to join them for a weekend in their cabin in West Virginia. It was a chance to get away from the chaos of our lives. While I deeply appreciated the respite, I also found that the feelings of grief and desperation followed me throughout the weekend. I felt like I was swimming in a dark cloud. As often happens, I eventually decided that the difficult weight of my emotions wasn't going to go away unless I made a decision to take on a new outlook. My husband and I took a walk through the cold woods before we left, to catch one last moment of peace together. I told him that we needed to do something different to cope with our new circumstances. We both agreed. "Let's be Buddhas," I said. "Let's," was his reply.

For us, Buddhism's approach to life and death makes sense. It relies on an acceptance of the way things are and the impermanence of everything, including us and our world. The story about the time that Mark Epstein, Jack Kornfield and other young westerners asked the great Thai Buddhist teacher Achaan Chaa about the fundamentals of Buddhism is one of my favorite descriptions of the Buddhist perspective. From Epstein and Kornfield's retelling of the story, Achaan Chaa smiled and picked up his water glass explaining that to him the glass was already broken. He went on to say that he enjoyed drinking out of the glass, that it held water quite well, that it reflected light beautifully. But, he said, when it inevitably gets knocked off the table or falls from the shelf, then his response would be, "Of course." When we understand that the glass is already broken every moment with the glass becomes precious.

We weren't entirely sure how to go about becoming Buddhas, but we figured it might start with meditation. So we devoted time every day to meditating: sometimes together, sometimes alone, sometimes sitting on our cushions, sometimes lying in bed before we went to sleep. We just tried to start fitting it in, tried to start calming some of the clutter in our minds and quietly be with ourselves and the tremendous weight that life had placed on us. I also began reading books, like Jack Kornfield's *Wise Heart,* as guidance and support for this journey I was on.

Eventually, we decided to sign up for a week-long silent retreat at the Bhavana Society in West Virginia. In typical retreat procedure, we would take a vow of silence for seven days. During those days, we would eat only breakfast and lunch. We would rise early and go to sleep early.

As we approached the retreat center, I thought about the first time Andrew had gone on a week-long silent meditation retreat. I recalled saying that I would rather break my leg than spend a week silently meditating. Now, while nervous, I also remember feeling like this retreat felt like air: an absolute necessity for my survival. I sat down on my cushion and prepared for a week of getting really uncomfortable and really in touch with the darkness that was swirling inside.

What I found, somewhat quickly, was that instead of swirling darkness, a certain lightness took over. Every day I was only focused on whatever task was right in front of me. Sometimes that was eating, or showering, or making tea, or drinking tea, or cutting vegetables while on kitchen duty, or walking through the woods to my dorm. Often it was meditating. Somewhat unexpectedly, I was not sitting and contemplating my own death or my treatments or how we would afford those treatments or whether or not what

I was eating was fueling or killing the cancer. I was much more likely to be focused on how cold I felt, how much my back hurt, or how obnoxious it was that the guy next to me wouldn't stop clearing his throat and shuffling around. I had found relief from the weight I was under and it came in the form of just being, right there in the moment.

In those moments, I was alive. I was not dead. I was not dying. I was not cancer. I was not cancer treatments. I just was. I was breathing. I was being. There was nothing about that moment that was scary, nothing bad, nothing wrong. The moment just was. The moment was something that was always there, just waiting for me to recognize it; just waiting for me to be present in it.

In addition to this important realization, I also had some deeply connecting and beautiful meditations, especially towards the end of the week, as my mind quieted further. Among the most profound meditations for me were the simple Metta (loving kindness) meditations. In traditional Metta meditation you repeat a series of phrases, honoring yourself, then people you care about. You can then move to people who are challenging to you, or to the whole city, the whole state, the whole country or the whole world. There is no right or wrong way. The phrases I repeated during the retreat were along the lines of, "May I be happy. May I be peaceful. May I be safe."

I began by sending myself all of the love and compassion I could muster, truly wishing happiness, peace, and safety for myself. I would then move on to each individual in the room. I often didn't know their names, since we weren't speaking, but I would think: "Woman with awesome hair: May she be happy. May she be peaceful. May she be safe." I would then move on to all of the people I was closest to, and then all of my more distant friends and family. I repeated this phrase in my mind for each person I could think of and sent them each loving energy. Eventually, I would end with sending all of the people in the surrounding area loving kindness, and then in the state, and so on until I was sending loving kindness to the whole world. I think the giving side of myself really connected with the compassion and love that comes out of Metta meditation. But I also think that creating a space of such deep concentration connected me to my own mind in new and seemingly magical ways. On several occasions, after about an hour of Metta meditation, I found that my mind became this beautiful space filled with a deep, rich, peaceful love, a pure connectedness and a quiet like I had never experienced and haven't experienced since.

These experiences of discovering my mind-body connection and the power of the present moment have given me a sort of faith. I don't know what lies ahead for me, but regardless of what happens with my cancer I know I will go through pain and suffering: because I am human and that is a part of the human experience. But I also know that as long as I am alive, there are two places I will always have with me to help me find peace: my body and this moment. We all have those two things, and as long as we are humans living our lives we can always turn to them in a time of need.

It requires some practice, but only in so far as we can find peace much *quicker* and more easily if we've been practicing. But in many ways, these practices require no skill or experience. We can spend fifteen minutes or sixty minutes on the cushion every day, being good yogis, and that can have a profound impact on our physical and mental wellness. But we can also just stop, connect, and let go anytime we need to. That is the beauty of being mindful.

BODY

Often we see our bodies for all that they can't do. We aren't super models or Olympic athletes or we just can't shake this cold. But our bodies are incredible machines capable of taking us on great adventures. Our bodies are our source of consciousness and life. Connecting to our bodies and relating to them from a space of gratitude and compassion allows us to have a whole new relationship with ourselves and our world.

Courage Club Rule #5:

NOURISH YOUR BODY

"Eating well is a form of self-respect."

UNKNOWN

I would like to begin with a confession: my favorite food in the whole world is macaroni and cheese.

This feels like a secret, worthy of confession, for many reasons. In our foodie culture, macaroni and cheese isn't the most "grown up" of food options — especially because I'm not even talking about the kind that *would* count as grown up. I don't need my mac and cheese baked, or dressed with parsley or served in a tiny dutch oven. I'd go for the boxed stuff any day. The sense of confession also comes into play because I'm generally a pretty strict vegan who doesn't eat cheese and rarely eats pasta – so mac and cheese is breaking all of my own rules. Finally, aren't we all supposed to be pretending we love kale? I'm sorry, but I just do not like kale. I can let it slide in chip form, but I'm not writing home about a kale salad anytime soon.

So if you asked me what my favorite food is I would answer, possibly sheepishly, mac and cheese. Often this is the only question we get asked about our food. "What's your favorite?" And we tend to think about food primarily from a place of our likes and our dislikes — or as we grow older, from a place of calories and carbs. But food is about so much more than what tastes good and what doesn't, or how many calories it has. Food is a deep and fundamental part of every day of our lives. The food we eat actually becomes us: it provides the building blocks for every cell in our bodies. Food is the basis of civilization, the basis of culture. Food can make us happy when we are celebrating. It can comfort us when we are sad. Food is the source of life.

Despite all of the ways in which food is deeply a part of who we are, many of us would describe our relationship with food as complicated. I know I did for many years, and frankly, I probably still would some days. We might love to eat, to cook, to bake, and even to grow food, and yet there remains a disconnect in our minds about what we want and what we *should* want. We want to crave kale, but we crave cake. We want to make good decisions, but sometimes the decisions can be overwhelming.

My relationship with food was complicated before cancer. For many years I suffered from hypoglycemia, which meant whenever I ate sugar I would experience severe crashes that sometimes resulted in full body tremors. To combat this, I put myself on extremely strict diets, most of the "low-carb" variety, which were quite fashionable at the time. In retrospect, this basically meant I was eating meat and cheese, with some vegetables. It probably wasn't terribly nutritious, but it did help my hypoglycemia a great deal. I still wanted desserts in my life, however, which meant I was constantly searching for some artificially sweetened treat that usually left me feeling miserable.

I eventually gave up meat, after watching the movie *Food, Inc.*, but it was still a struggle to keep my weight down. I wasn't chubby, but if I ate poorly I could easily pack on the pounds. I was therefore constantly trying to eat the "right" thing: seeing carbs and sugar as the enemy, protein as the ally and really nothing much else when I thought about food. I ate thinking about little other than weight, either because I was restricting myself to try and keep extra weight off, or because I was feeling guilty that what I was eating would mean I'd gain a few extra pounds.

When I was diagnosed with cancer, food took on a totally new meaning. A new option opened up to me. I could, and should, eat to fight cancer. There were whole categories of cancer-fighting foods. There were also whole categories of cancer-causing foods. There were dozens of studies on which diets led to higher rates of cancer, which diets decreased those rates, which diets increased risk of recurrence, which diets decreased that risk. And few were totally consistent. I had a world of overwhelming and sometimes conflicting new information.

One decision I made early on was to become vegan. Multiple studies showed the benefits of reducing or eliminating animal fats for triple negative breast cancer. I also took a much stronger stance against sugar, as I feared that sugar would feed my cancer. It's well known that cancer metabolizes sugar faster than any other cells in our body. I couldn't help but think about the cancer cells gobbling up the glucose anytime I ate anything sugary. I also tried to incorporate more fruits and vegetables in my diet, as they cover the vast majority of cancer-fighting foods. Now, instead of just wondering whether or not I liked something, or whether or not something would make me gain weight, I now considered how food would impact my health.

Going through chemotherapy made me deeply averse to feeling sick, so I began to think a lot about how food made me feel. On the rare occasion that I would cheat and eat something I shouldn't, I often realized that I didn't feel well afterward. I was taken back to high school and the first time that I realized I felt really bad after eating a fast food hamburger. How many times had I felt this bad and not given it a second thought?

While I was on cancer treatments I was able to stick to my diet pretty well. Once treatments were over, however, it became increasingly difficult to keep eating healthy. By the time the holidays rolled around I was cheating, breaking all of my rules, having way too much sugar and candy and holiday goodies. When I had my recurrence, I became convinced that it was my fault. I hadn't stuck with my diet. I had been feeding the cancer. So I did what any afraid-out-of-their-mind person would do. I stopped eating. I was terrified of food. I ate only the bare minimum to keep myself upright all day. The sick, anxious feeling in my stomach made food pretty unappealing anyway.

Slowly, as I started to find treatment options and became a little less anxious, I started to come back to food. As I did, I went through wild swings. Some days I would be perfectly happy whipping up all kinds of complicated cancer-fighting concoctions. Other days I would get bitter and angry that I couldn't eat what everyone else was, and I would eat whatever I wanted. This was almost always followed by days of feeling guilty about what I had eaten. I was constantly beating myself up: except this time, it wasn't because I thought I wouldn't lose weight. It was because I thought I wouldn't survive.

Making my relationship with food a life or death situation was not ideal, to say the least. Food is everywhere. It is deeply embedded in our social activities. It is in our traditions. It brings us together. My complex feelings about food, the constant guilt I felt for never eating "perfectly," the fear I had about my moments of weakness: they all made me never want to leave the house. Social gatherings became painful exercises in self-control. Dinners out were sometimes an embarrassing affair of discovering how many items could be removed from my order ("No cheese, or butter, oh, and no bread!") Food was making my life miserable.

I knew I had to make a change when my husband got teary-eyed one day after I flew into a rage about how terribly I'd been eating and how I was killing myself. "I just wish I could have macaroni and cheese every once in a while!" I exclaimed. He teared up and said, "I wish you could, too." It made me incredibly sad for both of us to think that my poor husband was brought to tears over my anxiety about food.

I realized that my judgmental approach to my own eating habits wasn't serving me well, and it certainly wasn't serving my health well. I had to reconnect with food in order to reconnect with myself and my life. I began to look at food as a source of nourishment. Instead of asking, "How might this food make me gain weight?" or "How might this food make my cancer grow?" I started looking at food through the lens of health and nutrition. How will this food feed my cells? How will it provide the nutrients I need? How will it keep inflammation low? How will it make me physically feel? How will I emotionally feel as I eat it?

I try to keep all of these questions in perspective. The first three, about feeding my cells, providing me nutrients, and lowering inflammation, all led me away from highly processed foods and towards nutrient-dense, organic fruits and vegetables. The beauty of these foods is that we can grow them with our own two hands; there aren't that many steps between the sun, the ultimate source of life, and our bodies; and they are delicious, despite what your inner five-year-old might be telling you.

The next thing I think about is how food makes me feel physically. So often our bodies are trying to tell us something by responding to the food we are eating. I remember just accepting that I would feel sluggish after eating a lot of meat, that I would feel sick after eating too much sugar, and that I would feel just generally awful after overstuffing myself at Thanksgiving. I now try to pay attention to how food makes me feel, and react accordingly. If I start to feel sick or out of balance, I back off. Sometimes even healthy food isn't right for our bodies at a particular time of day: maybe the fruit is too acidic or the vegetable has too much fiber. I try both to listen and respond, to give my body not just what tastes good but also what feels good.

And finally, it's important not to ignore how food makes me feel emotionally. As I confessed, I love mac and cheese. It comforts me, and sometimes I need comforting. I don't try and belittle myself for the possibly questionable choices I might make when I'm feeling stressed, or sad, or overwhelmed, or even if I'm just feeling celebratory. I give myself breaks. I try to keep relatively healthy options around the house, like a no-sugar-added coconut milk chocolate ice cream when an ice cream binge comes calling. But some days I just need to break all the rules and let myself indulge. When that happens, I try to acknowledge what's happening. "I see you grief. It's okay that you're here. Here's a pizza." Instead of feeling guilty afterward, compounding the negative emotions that made me want to comfort myself with food in the first place, I acknowledge that I found a way to give myself a little comfort and self-compassion when I needed it.

For a long time, I had thought of food as something external to myself, separate from who I am as a person, something I had to battle with constantly. Ultimately, I have learned that food is an integral part of who I am, how I engage with the world, and how I feel both emotionally and physically. Now I try to connect to it from a space of loving-kindness, a space that wants to nourish my body as much as it wants to feed it, that wants me to feel good and well and taken care of. This idea has revolutionized my relationship with food. At the end of the day, we literally become what we eat, physically. Emotionally, we become the emotions we attach to our food. We can either live in a state of constant guilt or we can live in a place of well-being. Let's be self-care rock stars and give our bodies and our minds the love they need, through the food we put on our plates every day.

Courage Club Rule #6:

MOVE YOUR BODY

"I started to move my body and I felt
so much better."

NELLY ODESSA

My body is an amazing miracle machine, capable of feats of resilience that would blow your mind.

If I had read this line a few years ago I would have laughed. "Not MY body! My body is full of flaws; it isn't even capable of losing three pounds, let alone being a miracle machine." Before cancer, my relationship with my body was primarily confrontational. I had an idea of what a body should look like, how strong a body should be, and what a body should be able to accomplish; my body was none of those things.

From a pretty early age, the general consensus was that my body lacked a certain level of coordination. As I got a little older and my friends started playing sports, I joined in, but I was a long shot from being the star player. In high school, I played volleyball, tennis and softball, and the overwhelming feeling I had most of the time was: don't embarrass yourself. I always felt like I had to work extra hard just to play at an average level.

As I moved into my adult years, my solution for the discomfort I had with my body was to push it as hard as I could. I began a weekly workout routine that involved spending over an hour at the gym on a regular basis. It felt good to sweat, to push my body to new limits, to constantly overcome pain to reach a new level. I also started riding my bike everywhere; no amount of cold, rain or sweltering weather could make me stop pushing myself. I couldn't understand my friends who went to yoga every day. I didn't want to connect with my breath; I wanted to be *out* of breath. I didn't want the slow burn of a stretching muscle, but the red-hot burn of a muscle about to be worn out. I didn't want my workout to relax and center me; I wanted my workout to physically exhaust me. "No pain, no gain" was definitely my mantra.

And then, with cancer, something new began to happen. I didn't have the energy or the stamina for the kind of intense workouts I had been doing. I no longer had the desire to push my body as hard as I could, because I knew my poor body was already getting beaten up by all the procedures, tests, and chemo that I was putting it through. At first, I would go for a run simply because I needed a break from the overwhelming emotions that a cancer diagnosis brought with it. On days when I was feeling afraid, I would put on my "be brave" mix and go outside to just run, allowing myself the space to feel powerful and rooted in my strength and movement.

Later, I would go running in celebration. When I was recovering from chemotherapy and felt good enough to go for a run, even if it was slow with lots of breaks, it felt like a triumphant act just to have the energy to put one foot in front of the other. I praised my body's resilience.

Then there were the days when my body physically and emotionally needed to move. These were the times when trauma was just beginning its cruel march into my nervous system and I needed to release the energy that my Autonomic Nervous System was building up.

For instance, when I got the news that my previous twelve rounds of chemotherapy had not worked, I felt this fight, flight or freeze mode take over. My rational brain shut down and all I could feel *was fear:* overwhelming, blindsiding, body rocking fear. I tried to continue with my day, tried to accomplish at least one small task, but the adrenaline kept pumping. And so, I put on my shoes, and I ran. It was raining, I was bald and I was sobbing, but I had one of the best runs of my life. My body needed to release the energy that was building up. If I didn't let this release happen, the trauma would imprint and live on in my body.

So in many ways, my body was learning to cope, by allowing the fear and trauma to move right through it.

Running became a tool for me: not just to love and celebrate my body, but to physically release fear and trauma. Moving and exercising became an extension of my emotions, a new way to feel, invite, and release the complex daily feelings associated with cancer. As I began daily physical therapy after my double mastectomy, I noticed that the work of stretching, opening and releasing pain from my body was helping me to be more emotionally vulnerable. I began to notice all the ways in which I moved and held myself, and to see them as clues to my own emotional well-being. My body instinctively wanted to cower inward, hunch down around my painful places, sleep with arms wrapped around my broken middle. I began to practice yoga in addition to physical therapy, as a way to practice stretching, opening and releasing both my body and the emotional turmoil I faced. I was discovering an intense emotional intelligence that lived beneath my skin; as long as I listened to it and paid attention, I could learn a great deal.

As I came to the end of my first-year of treatments, I had no idea how powerful and important my newfound connection to my body would become. The end of treatments, when I was initially in remission, was an extremely difficult time for me. I felt more disconnected from my own emotions than I had in a long time. I'd been waiting for this day for an entire year, waiting for the treatments to be behind me, and life to be ahead of me. I was supposed to be excited, and yet, I found myself terrified of what this new life of mine might bring. Would the cancer return? Would it eventually kill me? The fear was overwhelming. The more I dug back into my life, and the more I built a future for myself, the more I felt cancer could take it away if it did return.

On top of that, cancer had stripped away so much of my identity that I no longer knew who I was. I knew Katie-before-cancer; I knew Katie-as-a-cancer-patient; Katie-after-cancer was a totally new person. I couldn't just pretend that the last year hadn't happened, but I also didn't want the rest of my life to be defined by cancer. I was truly and deeply lost for the first time in my life.

It was at this precise moment of feeling confused and overwhelmed that I embarked on a trip with First Descents. First Descents is an outdoor adventure program that offers free, week-long trips of surfing, kayaking or climbing to young adult cancer survivors and fighters. I signed up to go rock climbing with them in Moab, Utah.

Arriving at the airport in Moab, I was a ball of nervous energy. I didn't know if I'd get along with the other cancer fighters and survivors. I didn't know if I'd be able to be myself, or even figure out who that self was. And mostly, I was afraid I wasn't strong enough to get up that rock.

By the end of the first night in Moab, I knew I had nothing to be afraid of when it came to my fellow cancer fighters and survivors. They got me. They got my hang-ups, my fears, my dreams, my aches and my pains. I felt safe and understood around them in a way that I hadn't since I was diagnosed. They were also fearless and determined. I watched them as they climbed the rocks without hesitation, getting banged up and cut up as they went, just powering onward and upward. They gave me the inspiration to believe that I could do the same.

My first few climbs were exhilarating. My body wasn't perfect, but it was getting me up those rocks. I wasn't failing, wasn't falling; I was reaching the top, to be rewarded with incredible views of the Colorado River against burnt orange sandstones for as far as the eye could see.

It was on the second day, however, that I really discovered the beauty of what First Descents can do for your soul.

I'd decided to tackle what looked like a relatively difficult climb. There was a small ledge halfway up, and I'd consoled myself with the idea that I should be able to climb at least to the ledge, and could turn back there if need be. When I got to the ledge, however, I decided I wanted to go all the way. (Plus, I don't think my chorus of supporters above and below me would have let me back down so easily.)

So, I started my way up the second half of the climb. It was difficult, but I was getting creative, finding ways to scoot myself up, scrounging for every inch I could get. It wasn't until about three feet from the top that I realized my muscles were completely spent. My legs and arms were shaking and I could not, for the life of me, reach the last big hold to pull myself to the top. I took several breaks, letting myself be held by the ropes while I tried to get my body ready to give it a go once again. I would rest, come back, and spend several minutes trying to work my way out, only to have my muscles fail me once again. I was getting increasingly desperate, wishing more and more that I could just quit. I didn't see how I could possibly overcome this painful and difficult slump I'd gotten myself into.

Fortunately for me, I had a friend just a few feet away at the top, and she was not about to let me give up. I finally realized that I just had to dig deep and find the strength to keep going. I took a moment and allowed myself to pull up my most painful memories from the previous year. I thought about all of the physical pain I had endured against my will. I thought about the uncomfortably long days spent just trying to survive another round of chemotherapy. I thought about the moments in the hospital recovering from my double mastectomy, and how hard I had to concentrate to live through the pain. I felt a hard-won resilience coursing through my veins. If I could endure that pain, *against* my will, then I could endure this pain.

I got back on the rock and this time, instead of being afraid of the pain and pulling back from it, I went into it. I allowed myself to really feel the strain in my muscles, to deeply experience the stress on my body. I used my knowledge of my own resilience to move through the pain, to move beyond it, to find those last few inches until my hand could grab onto that last big hold. In a moment of complete and utter relief I grabbed onto the hold and pulled myself up.

I have rarely felt so accomplished in my life. I conquered so much more than just a difficult climb that day.

I found myself through my body on that trip. Before it, I hadn't understood just how resilient I'd become. Because of what I'd endured mentally and emotionally, I was now *physically* more capable. I had wondered who I was after cancer. How could I be someone who had cancer but was not defined by it? I found my answer out on that rock. Cancer had shaped me for the better. It had made me a stronger, braver, hardier version of my former self. It had given me this well of emotional, mental and physical resilience that could not be taken from me. And most importantly, it had taught me to connect to my body in completely new ways.

I now see my body as an extension of my mind and my emotions. When I'm feeling overwhelmed by emotions, I can now turn to my body as a resource. I can ask my body where it feels the emotion, and by allowing myself to physically feel fear or anger I can much more easily let it go. If my body needs to move in order to find that release, I will move it. And I turn to yoga and more contemplative mind-body practices when I know that there is angst living in my bones or when I know my mind needs stretching as much as my muscles do.

These days I am much less harsh on my body. I work out to connect, to feel alive, or to work something out, not because I'm chasing some ideal that I'll never reach. I hold a deep appreciation for the way my body allows me to feel, allows me to experience and allows me to live in this world. In this way my connection with my body has allowed me to create experiences that are much more meaningful than another day at the gym. By moving in a way that is connected to my emotions, my resilience and my courage I am creating experiences that change the way I see myself and my world.

My body is an amazing, miracle machine, capable of feats of resilience that will blow your mind.

Courage Club Rule #7:

BE YOUR BODY'S ADVOCATE

"Health is a relationship between you
and your body."

TERRI GUILLEMETS

Right before my thirtieth birthday, I suddenly decided that I was in desperate need of a physical exam and that I needed to find a primary care physician stat. It may seem irresponsible to be 29 years old and not have a PCP, but who has the time to care about things like your health when you're 29? On the whole, it seemed much easier to ignore any aches and pains and wait for my invincible body to make them magically go away. But somewhere around 29 and 10 months, I suddenly felt the urge to know the inner workings of my body. I chalked it up to my brain getting smarter about my health. It wasn't until after the fact that I realized it was actually my body that had coaxed my brain into the doctor's office that day.

After conducting thorough research, I found a PCP that seemed right up my alley — but when I called the office he couldn't see me for months. I settled for the nurse practitioner. There is nothing wrong with nurse practitioners, and absolutely nothing wrong with seeing a female instead of a male, but there most definitely WAS something wrong with this *particular* nurse practitioner.

She was probably in her mid-fifties, and burst into the room in a too tight mini-skirt and very low cut blouse. She cursed three times in the first few sentences of her opening monologue. I call it a monologue because I didn't get to say much for the first five minutes or so. I wouldn't go so far as to call it rehearsed: it was primarily a mixture of cursing, bemoaning the cruelties of aging and time, repeating how jealous she was of my youth, and lecturing me on how to stay ahead in the fast-paced culture of DC life. One thing I had liked from her profile was that she had studied stress reduction techniques; when I asked her about them, her advice was: "Most people in this city are too busy for actual stress reduction, so I just prescribe most of my patients Valium. I take at least two or three a day myself. Shall I write you a prescription?"

"Umm, no thank you," was my timid response. I knew this lady was crazy, but I wasn't nearly as horrified as I should have been. Back then I saw doctors as the experts and myself as the uneducated patient who had better do what they told me. I did know enough to easily conclude I didn't need Valium to cope with stress and that, furthermore, I probably didn't want to be taking medical advice from a potty-mouthed, over-caffeinated, under-dressed, muscle-relaxant addict who claimed to be a promoter of "health" and "wellness."

A few days later, after looking at my blood work, this is the woman who would diagnose me with Graves' disease. A few days after that, I would go from being generally asymptomatic to living with full-blown, can't-get-out-of-bed immune system disorder.

Looking back, it wasn't a coincidence that I was getting a physical exam and blood work just weeks before my body was about to give out. My body was crying out for help. I'd had a number of very strange symptoms for months that I hadn't consciously understood or put together. Exercise had become more and more difficult. I had begun having strange sleep problems, like sleep talking, waking up in a panic, and the embarrassing habit of drooling. Little did I know that these were all symptoms of a thyroid that was growing in both size and efficiency. I firmly believe that my seemingly random desire to get a physical was my body telling my brain, "Something is wrong here and we'd like to get our conscious self in on what's going down."

In the three years since then, being surrounded by doctors and medicine, diagnostic machines and lots of strange and sometimes scary symptoms has taught me how important it is to listen to my body, even when the "expert" is telling me I am wrong. When I found the lump near my clavicle I knew it was cancer. I visited my doctor and he told me it was nothing, definitely just a cyst on a blood vessel. As relieved as I was to hear that, I also didn't feel comfortable with his conclusion. I demanded an ultrasound, which led to a biopsy and a PET scan, which resulted in the diagnosis of my recurrence. I had been through my first three-month check-up less than a month before, and my cancer markers, the only thing they use to measure recurrence, were normal. Had I listened to my doctors I would not have caught my recurrence as early as I did.

Often our symptoms don't fit into the diagnostic tools the Internet has developed. Often we know the difference between something that may sound serious but is actually nothing, and something that sounds like nothing but is actually serious. For me this included things like the night-time drooling that ended up being an autoimmune disease; the terrifying heart attack symptoms that ended up being a slight swelling, easily cured by ibuprofen; the giant hard lump in my armpit that ended up being dying fatty tissue, not a tumor; the lump on my ovary that almost led to the removal of my ovaries when it was, in fact, just a cyst; and the blood vessel cyst that turned out to be Stage 4 cancer. When it was something bad I just knew it in my heart of hearts. When it was nothing, I wasn't ever too worried.

Of course, it's very easy to let people scare us and make us question our own instincts, but I got used to gut checking someone else's fear against my own intuition.

At the end of the day, I've learned that I am the number one expert and authority on my own body. Only I am with my body all day long. Only I know how I physically feel, know my symptoms inside and out. It is extremely easy to believe that those in health care know more than we do. They do, in some ways; depending on the type of doctor, they likely know more than we do about the human body, research, pharmaceuticals, or energy, chakras, acupuncture points, diet, herbs, etc. But no one knows *our* bodies better than we do. Nobody else gets direct communication from our bodies all day long in the form of cramps, pain, headaches, indigestion and more. We just need to listen.

The next most important thing I've learned on my medical odyssey: The doctors work for *you*. Oncologists can be a scary bunch. I don't think they mean to be, but they wield such tremendous power. Here's a complete stranger, who you meet in 15-minute intervals, who holds all the knowledge and all the power about your cancer. They get the information about your scans and pathology first, so they are the ones who know whether your news is good or bad. They have made the decisions about treatment protocols, so they tell you whether or not you need Treatment X, which can sometimes determine everything else about your life. They say, "You need four months of chemo" and you hear: "Cancel every plan you made for the next four months because I said so." They are the ones who tell you, once it gets bad, about how many months you might have left to live. Cancer can easily dictate everything about your life — and since oncologists are "in charge" of the cancer, so can they.

I let my doctors have a lot of power for a very long time. I really wanted to be the "good patient." I wanted my doctors to like me and think I was smart and easy to handle. This may just be an extension of my general life agenda to get people to like me. But there is something about a doctor and the authority that goes along with their position that especially makes me want to be on their good side.

But there were times when being the good patient became really difficult. It started out with the problems I had with bedside manner. The first time I cried in front of my very strict Brazilian oncologist was when my latest MRI showed that the chemotherapy had been ineffective at shrinking my tumor. This was particularly disturbing because a previous MRI had shown there had been shrinkage; I was told it had been read wrong. I was trying to understand how this could have happened, and I began to tear up as I watched my oncologist shrink back from me, rigid and uncomfortable. And then she said the most robotic thing I have ever heard another human say: "Your fear is just a symptom of the MRI."

I was not being treated like a human. I was being treated like a case file. Every week I came to her with my complaints. "My mouth is filled with sores." She told me the chemo was destroying the lining of my mouth and I got "magic mouth-wash" to briefly numb the pain. "I have an itchy rash all over my body." She told me I was allergic to the experimental drug and I got prescription strength anti-itch cream. "I feel nauseated at night." She told me the chemo was destroying my stomach lining and I got a sleeping pill that fights nausea. "I'm terrified that this MRI shows the treatments aren't working and that means the cancer is going to kill me." She told me it was a symptom of the MRI and if I was just more rational, I would feel better.

Eventually, when I finally got over my "be a good patient" mentality, I found a new oncologist who listened to me and didn't try to tell me how I was feeling. This was an enormous step for my physical and emotional health. When you are living with a chronic illness like cancer, it's critical to have a team of health care providers who treat you like a partner, a human, and not like a set of symptoms, a disease, or an emotionless robot. Understanding that patients are human requires taking time to understand the full person. It's true that many medical professions are set up for expediency, not for spending time getting to know patients. That just means you have to find the doctor who is willing to give you the time and sensitivity you deserve in the face of the pressures of their industry.

You want your doctor to listen to you because they are *your* consultant. They are working for you. When I was diagnosed with a recurrence, I couldn't find a single doctor who said, "We can help you." Most told me they had nothing for me. So I kept talking to doctors until I found one who said, "Yes, I can help." He was the 18th or 19th doctor I'd spoken to, an independent oncologist, outside of the traditional medical system, and while he is expensive, he also spends no less than an hour with me every time I see him. This gives us plenty of time to discuss my case, my life, and my options. He gives me research articles and I read them to decide if a new treatment sounds promising. I give him research articles and he reviews them to see if he feels comfortable with the treatment I am proposing. It's a partnership. This is what all doctor-patient relationships should be like.

These kinds of relationships can be difficult to find in traditional systems. It depends highly on the personality of the doctor. For your health, it's worth going the extra mile to find the gem. Even if you aren't in a health crisis now, it's helpful to consider whether your doctor is the person you would want delivering life-altering news, or supporting you through your most difficult journeys.

There are some medical disciplines where this kind of ideal patient-doctor relationship is much easier to find. In addition to my oncologists, I also have a therapist, a Reiki master, a Rolfer, a chiropractor, a naturopath, a nutritionist, a Qi Gong teacher, a physical therapist, several acupuncturists, and more. Practitioners in these realms, while they rarely take health insurance, should be able to spend time with you and listen to you. The really good ones should have such strong intuition that it feels like you are meeting with a psychic. Finding these people has helped me to see my health and wellness from many angles. Sometimes the remedy isn't medicine. Sometimes it's movement, meditation, herbs or an adjustment.

At the end of the day, we only have this one body and this one life. Our bodies are constantly speaking to us, telling us what they really need, and alerting us when something is wrong. We owe it to them to trust those moments of intuition. We also owe it to them to find the professionals who are willing to be our partners in health. Medicine can be deeply disempowering, especially for the patient. But we can fight for those spaces of empowered health and wellness. We can find the good doctors that don't make us feel the need to be "good patients." By being an advocate for our bodies and our health we can find a new form of wellness and connection to our bodies and our own power to heal ourselves.

WORLD

The world around us has the potential to bring tremendous inspiration and meaning to our lives. Once we've deeply connected with ourselves, we are ready to connect with our world: through the causes we care most about, through exploration of all this planet has to offer, and through the people in it.

Courage Club Rule #8:

CONNECT TO A CAUSE

"You only fight well for causes you yourself have shaped, with which you identify–and burn."

RENÉ CHAR

For a long time I thought that meaning in life came from pursuing, deeply and passionately, one narrowly focused purpose. As a kid I couldn't wait to grow up and discover my purpose, my reason for being here. I assumed my purpose would become my career and I assumed that career would be in service of some great cause. When I was young and idealistic, I believed that this purpose of mine would be more important than anything else in my life and that if I didn't dedicate myself to it 120% that I wouldn't really be doing it right. I also believed that there was some great magical formula that could take someone's favorite cause and favorite activities, combine them, and spit out the perfect career.

My first great cause came as a high school senior, when I had the opportunity to develop a relationship with several communities in Malawi where I started a small non-profit, with the help of my family, to raise money for community development. It became immediately apparent that I wanted to devote my life to this cause of supporting impoverished communities through their own empowerment. All throughout college, I organized people and events, pulling together fundraisers and inspiring people. Not only did I love doing it, I also like to think I wasn't half bad at it either.

After graduating from college I really wanted to join the Peace Corps, but made a deal with my boyfriend and future husband that we would do his thing first for two years. His thing was being in Teach for America in Philadelphia. So I got a job as an AmeriCorps volunteer teaching community service to 18-21-year-old high school dropouts in inner city Philadelphia. I loved my students. I would have done almost anything for them. The challenges they faced broke my heart on an almost daily basis. But I knew by the time my two years ended that this was not my cause. When I looked at the challenges of American education, I didn't feel hopeful or inspired or motivated: I felt completely overwhelmed. When I thought about teaching, I felt the same way. I am not a born teacher and education is not my cause. And that's ok. I wouldn't trade my experience as a teacher for anything, and it was honestly difficult to leave my students, to move away from being in direct contact with such incredible humans every day. But I knew it wasn't what my heart or my mind could bear to do for the rest of my life.

After my experience in AmeriCorps, I moved on to the Peace Corps: the dream job, in my mind. Just a few months after our wedding, my husband and I began our Peace Corps adventure in Tonga, a small group of islands in the middle of the South Pacific. After a few months, though, I started to get severely depressed. I had been sick pretty consistently over the first few months, and my illness, combined with being provided with very little work or direction, made me feel rather useless in this new job. Andrew and I returned home after just seven months of Peace Corps service, and I felt like an enormous failure having not succeeded at this life-long dream of mine.

We moved to Washington, DC next, and I decided to pursue a career in international development policy. My experiences in Malawi were still near and dear to me, but my experiences in both AmeriCorps and the Peace Corps had taught me that direct service might not be my sweet spot. Fortunately, I had been given the opportunity, in college and while living in Philadelphia, to try my hand at advocacy work. I'd discovered that I really loved the thrill of convincing America's leaders to do the right thing (or at least not the wrong thing) for people living in poverty around the world. I enjoyed, and felt like I had a talent for, this kind of engagement. I liked sussing people out, trying to meet them where they were at, finding the argument that would convince them, and getting to see policies and positions take formation that I knew would do some good in the world. I bounced around between organizations and eventually found *the* cause that I was going to devote my life to: food rights. As I was getting started in DC there was a massive global food crisis, and I became involved in doing lots of research and advocacy around how the world could tackle our inability to feed everyone. This was a cause that moved me deeply. I eventually found an organization that I felt deeply committed to, and settled into my career, loving every second of it.

When cancer came along, at first I was adamant that I wouldn't let it impact my career. Through my first year of treatments, I worked as much as I was physically able. When treatments were over, I had great plans to dive right back into my work and take on more than ever. I traveled a number of times that fall for work, took on some big challenges, and accepted a promotion.

When I had a recurrence and suddenly felt that my life might be cut very short, my work, this thing that I had determined I would devote my life to, immediately took a back seat. In an instant, I no longer cared about my job. Crisis has a way of making priorities crystal clear, and all of a sudden the thing I'd thought was my life's great purpose was no longer a priority. It's not that I no longer cared about the cause that my job was fighting for, but all of the meetings I had, the emails in my inbox, the reports that needed to be written, felt insignificant compared to the desperate need I felt to spend a little more time with the people I love. I took three months off from work, and when I did eventually go back it was only part-time.

All of a sudden my life's purpose was gone. Even though I was still working, it had become apparent that I would likely not be able to devote the rest of my life to fighting for this cause I cared so much about. There were more important things, like my family and friends and my health. At the time, I assumed I had been naïve to believe that I needed to devote my life to some singular purpose. Unfortunately, this assumption was also decidedly wrong.

After months of doing nothing but focusing on myself and my own health, my life began to feel very small. I craved connection to something bigger than myself. I was still working, but didn't have the time or energy to make the kind of impact I wanted to make in the complicated world of food rights policy. And so, slowly but surely, I began to find other places to engage.

I started working more with young adults cancer organizations. After a few years in the trenches, I felt like a bit of a veteran, with something to offer those coming after me. I started to share some of the health, wellness, and nutrition information I had been collecting since my cancer journey began. It felt good to know that I was helping others to get healthy and well, hopefully preventing terrible illnesses like the one I was experiencing. I started supporting petitions and advocacy to get funding for Stage

4 breast cancer. Organizations like MET UP are following the lead of AIDS organizations like ACT UP to demand more funding for research for Stage 4 breast cancer. Even though thirty percent of all breast cancers will metastasize, only seven percent of funding goes to researching metastatic breast cancer, which kills 40,000 Americans every year. Someday, Stage 4 cancer could and should be seen as a chronic disease and not a killer. It feels good to be part of the movement that can someday make this a reality, even if it will be too late for me.

Throwing myself back into these causes, being the advocate that I was at heart again, and putting my talents for organizing and inspiring people, raising money, and writing strongly worded letters to good use made me feel connected again to something bigger than myself. In the end, I don't think it's necessary for our lives to have *one* grand, important cause or purpose. But I do think it's important to connect to *some*thing larger than ourselves and our own lives.

When we think of our true nature as humans, we rarely think of empathy as being part of that. Indeed, as a species we are capable of great destruction. But research has shown that even chimpanzees are capable of empathy and selflessness. We may have selfish genes, but we also have empathetic genes that make us want to feel that we are contributing to something. So even in crisis, even in the moments when it's most critical for us to focus our energy on ourselves, we must also find those spaces where we can devote energy to something bigger. Whether that's a small act, like mowing a neighbor's lawn, or a great, valiant cause that has you marching on Washington, it doesn't matter. What matters is that the cause lights *your* heart on fire, and connects you to all the goodness this world has to offer.

Courage Club Rule #9:

GO OUTSIDE

"Look deep into nature, and then you will understand everything better."

ALBERT EINSTEIN

When I was a little girl we had a trampoline in our back-yard — and it was the greatest. I was a master of all kinds of jumps with all kinds of names we had invented. But one of my favorite things to do on the trampoline wasn't actually jumping. On quiet summer days when I was alone in the house, I would grab my Walkman and lay face down on the trampoline, with my head resting on my arms folded in front of me. Through the black mesh, I could see the tall grass below our trampoline. Lying down, suspended like I was above the ground, I could watch all of the drama of the normally invisible world below me unfold. It took a moment of concentration, but once my eyes adjusted I could see all of the incredible creatures leaping, squirming and flying around just beneath me. As a young, angsty teenager, it's almost as if my brain knew that taking this little respite and letting myself become consumed by nature was the perfect way to meditate, to reconnect, and to give my mind a break from its usual anxiety. All I had to do was go outside, into my own backyard.

That instinct to go outside followed me into the darkest and most difficult days of my cancer treatment as well. I am not a particularly outdoorsy person. I like being outside, but I'm also a bit of a curl-up-on-the-couch kind of gal. Still, there were a few occasions over the course of my cancer journey in which going outside felt like an absolute necessity. Often in really heated moments, ones where I couldn't physically stand the fear or sadness or anger that had overcome me, I would go outside so I could run. A treadmill would not have sufficed in those circumstances. Even though it was cold or rainy or snowing, being outside felt like freedom, and that was exactly what I needed in those moments. In some ways, embracing the elements helped me to embrace my own emotions.

Then there were the times when I got really bad news, and couldn't stand the thought of sitting with the new information inside my home for days on end. It was times like these that Andrew and I would immediately agree we needed to go camping.

My most memorable instance of us opting for the "camping cure" was the day of my very last chemo. I had finally come to the end of my surprise extra four rounds of chemo. We had big plans to get through this chemo, celebrate my birthday, and head off to the Caribbean for a much-deserved vacation before radiation. I went to the infusion center and had my blood taken, as usual, so I could have labs done to make sure I was well enough to get chemo. I then went downstairs for my appointment with my oncologist.

When she came into the room, she informed me that I was anemic. My counts were too low, as a result of treatments, for me to have treatment that day. I would probably have to wait at least two weeks. The only plans I had made all year, to celebrate the end of chemo, throw myself a birthday party and go on vacation, were about to be ruined. I was exhausted and overwhelmed by the degree to which my own life had been taken completely out of my hands. I pleaded with her, to no avail.

I'd expected to spend the weekend feeling incredibly sick after chemo. Now I had a whole weekend on my hands to dwell on the fact that everything I was looking forward to was being taken away. Andrew and I knew immediately that we should go camping.

There's something about camping that makes me feel so much more connected to myself, my mind, and my world. When you're camping, every small thing you do requires extra thought and intention. You can't just throw a pizza in the oven. You have to carefully plan your meals. You have to start the fire, prep the food, and cook it over an open flame. There isn't much that's more satisfying than eating something you just cooked with a fire you started.

And then there's nature, all around you. It allows for a meditative contemplation without the anxiousness that can sometimes overcome us when we try to sit and meditate at home. In nature, there are wonders to behold, trees to listen to, a breeze to notice, a mountain to stare at in awe.

This type of quieting of our normal worries and anxieties that happens in new environments, can also occur during travel. Discovering a new city, tasting a new food, or engaging with a new culture can all open up our minds and allow us to see our lives, our world and ourselves in completely new ways. For me, spending time outside and traveling are both critical ways that I have built a meaningful life after cancer. In fact, they are perhaps the two most important things I have done to reclaim my sense of aliveness.

Since I was diagnosed, I've been on some of the best adventures of my life. When my treatments ended I took a work trip to Rome, and tacked on one extra day at the end all for myself. I charted a many-miles-long trip around the city that took me through all of the major ancient archeological wonders. Between seeing the Colosseum, the Forum, and the Pantheon, I treated myself to a pizza and some gelato in one of Rome's many romantic street corner cafes.

My next work trip was to Johannesburg right before Thanksgiving. I convinced my husband to meet me there, and we took off for a week to Cape Town, the most beautiful city I have ever laid eyes on. We spent the week rock climbing and hiking up Table Mountain. There is nothing in the world like hiking or climbing up a mountain, and then turning around to get a stunning view of a city on the ocean. There are few places in the world with such a unique combination of beauty. We also went diving with great white sharks and snorkeling with seals, two unforgettable experiences. Then in December, we spent a week with our friends in Mexico, chasing turtles around the bay outside our doorstep and exploring ancient Mayan ruins.

These experiences make my life feel full and rich and adventurous. Cancer can often feel very much like a trap. Treatments lock you into a specific schedule so you can never stray too far from the hospital. The treatments can also weaken you, making it hard to take on all of the adventures you want to. Scans every few months or every few years make you feel like you can't plan anything beyond that date, because the scan results could change everything. To be able to embrace the world, despite all of these restrictions, feels like escaping from the trap.

Probably my favorite adventure of any that I've taken was a trip to see gorillas in northern Rwanda. My best friend and work colleague, Meredith, and I had a work trip to Rwanda in the fall of 2015. We had never been on a work trip together, so we decided to tag on a few extra days of exploring. We quickly decided that, even though it was somewhat expensive, going to see the gorillas was a once in a lifetime experience we couldn't pass up. The cost is so high because the government of Rwanda wants to incentivize protecting the animals over poaching them, and the money goes back into conservation efforts.

Meredith and I took off from our hotel in Kigali and drove with Eric, our driver, through the breathtaking rolling Rwandan countryside before arriving at our inn, a collection of small but comfortable huts at the base of a string of volcanic mountains. The next day we put on our gorilla tracking gear and met up with our group. The trek itself was spectacular. We were hiking at a relatively steep incline through sometimes knee-deep mud in the middle of a bamboo forest that overlooked the beautiful Rwandan countryside.

Eventually, we came around a bush and there he was: George the gorilla, the dominant male of his family. All four-hundred-plus pounds of him were sitting there peacefully, chewing on some bamboo. I immediately welled up with tears. Gorillas had always been my favorite animal at the zoo, but seeing one just feet away from me in his native environment was a life-changing experience. We made the sound we'd been taught, to announce our presence and ask his permission to be there. It was a sort of deep, guttural "huh, huh" sound. We waited a moment and George made the sound back to us. I had spoken to a gorilla! We all know the joys of connecting with our pets, and the love we have for them. There is something special about that cross-species relationship. To see an animal in the wild, and to communicate with him, made me feel like I was deeply a part of the wild beauty of this planet.

We then heard a rustling sound, and saw some juveniles playing with each other. Two medium sized fluff balls were rolling around together wrestling, the way human kids do. Eventually our gorillas took off up the mountain, and we followed them in some of the steepest hiking I have ever done. We soon arrived at a flat clearing at the very top of the mountain. We were shaded by giant trees but could see mountain ranges and valleys on either side of us. In the clearing was the entire family. There were females with their babies, playing the way human children do. There were full-grown males who were in a constant mode of fighting for dominance. They fought and played and ate and mostly ignored us as we walked among them. It was the most incredible experience I have ever had in nature.

An experience like that stays with you for a lifetime. It changes you a little. When you return home you are now someone who knows that places like that exist on earth. Your mind has expanded a little. It's no wonder that people's bucket lists are never about things they need to buy. They are always places they want to see and experiences they want to have. Going outside, connecting to nature, being still in its presence, travelling, and seeing new things, all add to the incredible adventure that is life. When I look back on how I've spent my time on earth, these experiences of travel and adventure and time spent connecting to the beauty of the world are like bright little lights. They have made my life beautiful.

Recent studies have shown that people who regularly go on

hikes are more creative, healthier, and happier. Researchers don't completely understand all of the reasons why nature makes us happier, but I think many of us intuitively understand that it does. Perhaps it's our ability to be truly present when we're in nature or experiencing something new. In nature our senses are flooded, but not in the overwhelming way that Times Square might do. Rather, nature floods our senses with sensations that have been etched onto our genes by thousands of generations before us. Being in nature is natural. Connecting to nature can make us feel whole and complete. Exploring this vast and beautiful world makes us feel like we are a part of it. In the grand scheme of nature, we are simultaneously infinitely smaller than we can imagine — and also infinitely more miraculous and important than we will ever know.

Courage Club Rule #10:

LOVE

"Being deeply loved by someone gives you
strength, while loving someone deeply
gives you courage."

LAO TZU

When people are asked about what makes life meaningful, often the first thing that comes to mind is other people: our partners or spouses, our children, our parents, our friends, our families. It's other people that make life worth living. This is a fact that is very much engrained in our DNA. We are social mammals and require connection with other human beings: not just for our survival, but also for our own sanity and sense of well-being.

If this is the first thing that comes to mind when talking about a meaningful life, why save it for the very end of the book? Because all those things in between about connecting to ourselves, our bodies, and our world, make our connection to other people stronger and more meaningful. Nothing has taught me this better than the most important relationship in my life: the one I have with my husband.

Andrew and I met in what now feels like our childhood but was actually our senior year of college. Our meeting felt a little bit like magic, and that sense about our relationship has never faded. Andrew and I grew up about 15 minutes away from each other, but we met because of work we had both done on the other side of the world. One of Andrew's distant cousins was working at an orphanage in Malawi when Andrew decided he needed to take a semester off from college to figure out what he wanted to do with his life. He asked if he could join her, and spent a semester working with newborns, learning the Chichewa language, and becoming adept at killing and eating flying ants. About a year after Andrew had returned home I showed up at the same orphanage, where I was conducting research for my undergraduate thesis.

A family friend who had accompanied me on the trip and had coincidentally gone to high school with Andrew made the connection for us and pointed out that we both went to the same university. I found Andrew in my university's database and sent him an email. I remember writing the whole thing out and then having a real vulnerability attack, turning my computer off and slumping into bed to take one of my world-famous college cat naps. After lying down for a few minutes though, I jumped up, turned my computer on, hit send, and the rest is history. We would meet up a few weeks later. I think for both of us it was love at first meeting. I remember leaving his apartment that day with the overwhelming feeling that nobody in the world had ever understood me better. That feeling has never left me.

We started dating when we were twenty-one, moved in together nine or ten months after we met, got engaged a year later, and got married just over a year after that. By twenty-four, we were a happily married couple. Being so young, we had our fair share of growing pains, as the two of us figured out who we were as adults. Fortunately for us, we grew in the same direction.

When I was diagnosed with cancer, we were generally in a good place. We owned our own home and had a sweet little kitty we loved. Andrew was finishing up his Ph. D. and I was nearly done with grad school and had a great job. We felt lucky, and would often talk about how charmed our lives felt — and how we knew the bottom could drop out at any point. And then, of course, the bottom dropped out precipitously.

Cancer immediately threw our relationship into a whole new space, with entirely different roles and responsibilities. Overnight, Andrew became a caregiver and I became a patient. With Andrew's high tolerance for pain, and my knack for making chicken noodle soup and hawking

Vitamin C, we both knew these were not the roles that most naturally suited either of us. But we, like so many people in our situation, did the very best we could.

Andrew has really been a wonderful caregiver. He went with me to nearly every appointment; one of the perks of still being a graduate student was that his schedule was pretty flexible. He would sit and write his dissertation while I got chemo in the infusion center or recovered from chemo on what I began referring to as the "chemo couch." He would comfort me as I had breakdowns and disappointments. He practically lived at CVS for all the prescriptions he was constantly picking up for me. He made me food and shakes and always made sure I had everything I needed.

This does not mean, however, that the cancer did not take a tremendous toll on our relationship. There were many things that tugged away at our connection.

First, there was the sheer exhaustion of what we were going through. Every day was a battle, and we both were physically, emotionally, and mentally spent.

Second, we were constantly protecting each other. I tried to protect him from my darkest fears, my worst thoughts, my worst trauma, but sometimes this protection meant it all came bubbling up and exploded which was much more difficult for him to handle. He was, likewise, trying to protect me from *his* fears and worries. This generally meant that we couldn't lean on each other or share the tough thoughts and feelings that most needed sharing.

As time wore on and my coping mechanisms began to give out, I became more and more volatile, more difficult to handle, more explosive in ways that were often incomprehensible to Andrew and confusing even to myself. Andrew's coping mechanisms also wore thin, which meant he was less able to listen and support when he had such turmoil going on in his own mind. I found other friends who could support me, but that put a further strain on our relationship.

As my cancer treatments came to a close, we started seeing a therapist, knowing we needed some outside help to begin to bridge the gaps that cancer had carved between us. After one of these therapy sessions, we went out to dinner, and finally both admitted that each of us was afraid I was going to die. We had both been so afraid to even mention the word, both so scared we would just make the other feel more afraid. Yet it felt like such a relief to be able to talk about something that we both thought about all the time. Slowly but surely, as life moved back to a new post-cancer normal, our relationship began to overcome some of the bumps we had faced along the way. We started to come back to Katie and Andrew.

Little did we know that cancer was not finished transforming our relationship. After I was diagnosed with a recurrence, the two of us travelled around from hospital to hospital for several months, talking to doctors about my options. It seemed that my options were pretty limited, and after one meeting it finally hit home that we might not get to spend the rest of our lives together. We found the "meditation" space in the hospital, in between seeing different doctors — and we just held onto each other. For the next few months, we found it extremely difficult to let go. Suddenly, absolutely nothing else mattered. We became almost literally attached at the hip. On the couch, we were snuggled up against each other. Before we fell asleep we would hold onto each other. When he left the room I felt lonely, and he would complain whenever we were apart.

In our darkest hour a fierce love had turned on, like a light bulb whose switch had always been there. In everyday life, a relationship has plenty of highs and lows, with many more in-betweens. There are countless moments of frustration and annoyance, plenty of passive aggressive comments to make about dishes getting done and bills getting paid. Our partners rarely seem perfect, and in some relationships, partners are downright toxic. But when you find that really good love, when you work for commitment and communication, one person can light your entire world.

As we continue on our health odyssey, we continue to have our fair share of struggles. One thing we've tried to emphasize is that each of us needs to take care of ourselves. We've both been in therapy, both been doing the hard work to tackle the tough things that arise for us in our own lives and in our relationship together. I began working on my own feelings of self-worth because I realized that my lack of self-love was destroying Andrew. He has worked on the same, because he knew his insecurities were also tugging at our connection. We've worked on our ability to be vulnerable together, to accept the things that are most difficult to accept, to be mindful in our relationship. And we have celebrated our relationship, through food and travel and adventure.

For us, this means that we've reached a point where a lot of the egoistic entanglements that used to trip us up when we were younger are no longer there. We have been able to build a relationship in which we are both fully present, fully listening, fully loving one another and ourselves. Along my journey we have had moments of hope and elation, sometimes feeling like we might get to spend the rest of our lives together, but we have also had plenty of moments spent just trying to breathe in the love. We don't know how many moments we will get to have together, so we try and make even the mundane things special. We tell each other we love each other constantly. We thank each other for taking care of things around the house. We snuggle longer than we should. We try to support one another and be partners in every way we can.

And we don't ignore the scary stuff anymore. We talk about my death all the time. It might sound morbid, but for us it feels healthy. We are thinking about it anyway. I am currently living primarily for the love of this man, and I can only hope that the rest of my life and my death provide such a deep and lasting testament that he will feel it every day for as long as he lives. Before I married Andrew, I told him that my number one life goal was to learn how to love him perfectly. I am so happy to say that I know I can cross that one off the list.

Relationships are what make our world go around. My parents raised me in an incredible example of true and lasting love. They instilled in me the importance of having large communities, but small circles of friends. My brother taught me how love can evolve over a lifetime. My childhood friends have been there for almost three decades and have shown me the importance of a lifetime of loyalty. My best friends have been some of my life's greatest love stories, and eventually have just become an extension of my family. And my dog, Lucy, has taught me about what truly unconditional love looks like and what really fantastic snuggling should be all about.

Let us all be lucky enough to live lives filled with such love. Let us endeavor to build stronger connections to each other by building stronger connections to ourselves. Let us not take each other for granted. Let us take time each day to breathe in the love. And most importantly, let us remember that should you ever be told that the end of your life is near, nothing will matter anymore except the love you have for yourself and the people around you.

Final Thoughts

> "Life shrinks or expands in proportion
> to one's courage."
>
> ANAIS NIN

Before I leave you, I want to tell you about my friend Patrick. I only knew Patrick for a few months, but his life had a profound impact on mine. My husband and I had just moved to Frederick, Maryland, a busy, historic town between DC and Baltimore, when I met Patrick. He was a retired firefighter and solar panel salesman, around my age. We met after I signed up for a free solar panel consultation at my local Home Depot.

I was immediately at ease in Patrick's presence. It was clear he wasn't so interested in the role of salesman as much as he was interested in really making a difference, helping to create clean energy. Our conversation quickly turned from solar panels to our shared interests and passions. His eyes lit up when I told him I worked with poor farmers in Africa, and my eyes lit up when he talked about the organic farm he'd started with his wife Amanda on their property. We geeked out over agriculture and organic produce for a while, and as he packed up to leave for the day I silently set about scheming how I could become friends with my solar panel salesman.

A few days later I was pleasantly surprised to receive an email from Patrick, and not about solar panels. He had been thinking about expanding his career and wanted to know more about what I was doing internationally. I told him that I wanted to know more about starting a vegetable garden and we agreed to meet for lunch and exchange stories and expertise. We talked for two hours straight about agriculture and jobs, vegetable gardens and families, Frederick and solar panels. Patrick's main point that day was that he just wanted his life to make a difference; he wanted to contribute more to the world. He also wasn't afraid to talk to me about my life's challenges, about what it was like to face down my own mortality, about how to really live in the face of death. At the end of our lunch, we parted ways both inspired by our conversation and ready to dream big.

Patrick sent a note to thank me after our lunch and said the following:

I wanted to thank you for meeting me the other day, it was a very enlightening experience. Being in your presence is a neat thing. It is easy to recognize a loving and honest soul just looking to do the greater good. You are a good egg! I feel as though your entrance in my life may be a catalyst for more positive change. For that I thank you. The physical and emotional struggle you face is a daunting one but I hope you con-

tinue to bravely persevere. I don't want to be the guy that says "let me know what I can do to help?" and not follow through.

Patrick had taken the words right out of my mouth. True to form, Patrick made good on his promise to follow through. A few weeks later when our sink broke, I texted Patrick for information about local plumbers and he said, "I'll fix it!" Knowing that our medical bills made it difficult for us to afford a plumber, Patrick spent the next six hours fixing our sink, refusing to let us pay him with anything more than soup and cookies. Andrew and I were touched beyond words by Patrick's kindness. Knowing so few people in Frederick and having so few resources, Patrick had made us feel like we were at home — like we had people we could count on.

I would only see Patrick alive one more time, a few weeks later at our Christmas party. He would die a few months later in a single car accident, leaving behind his wife and their two young children.

I didn't know anyone who knew Patrick except his wife, and yet I could immediately feel the impact of his death all around me. The outpouring on Facebook was overwhelming. Everyone we spoke with anywhere we went in town had heard of his passing. Local restaurants and organizations immediately began raising money for his young family. The entire community was coming together, and even as one of its newest members I could see signs of the outpouring of love all around me. Patrick's funeral was no different. The enormous church was standing room only, with an overflow room and a live broadcast with hundreds of people watching.

It was this experience, as fleeting as it was, of meeting Patrick, getting to know him, being touched by his spirit and generosity and then losing him so suddenly that inspired me to write this very book. Why? Because we all deserve to have an overflow room at our funeral. Patrick didn't have an overflow room because of the way he *died*, suddenly and far too soon. Patrick had an overflow room because of the way he lived.

Patrick lived all in, completely devoted to making the most out of his life. He was self-less and totally committed to his family and friends. I saw that in the acts of kindness that Patrick bestowed upon us, but also in the outpouring of love for him and his family. Patrick also took the time to live a well-examined life. I could tell from our conversations how deeply Patrick considered his time here on earth. At his funeral, the eulogist read from his journal, in which Patrick contemplated his own death and how he would make a difference in the world. Patrick found peace and solace in his wife, his boys, his farm and in nature.

So many of us who have been through crises lose our ability to connect to our lives and live all in. We feel isolated and so our lives become isolating. Our pain and our suffering disconnect us from our bodies, our world and ourselves.

But life, this one life we have to live, is precious, no matter the devastation that has crossed our path. While some of us spend a great deal of time with death, *none* of us know when we may breathe our last breath. There is a way, a path, back to ourselves, to our bodies, to our worlds and it begins with courage. The root of the word courage is the Latin word *cor*, meaning heart. A courageous life is a life filled with love.

It begins with loving ourselves, our whole selves: our raw, vulnerable, imperfect, broken but brilliant selves. It ends with loving the people around us, as the imperfect and broken but brilliant people that *they* are. It requires constant practice — and in this case, practice will never make perfect. But practice will make a life: a big, bold, brave and beautiful life.

My life's work at this point is just to live, as much as I can, in whatever time I have left. I stumble every day, but I keep going, so that someday when I die, whenever that may be: "I will," as someone once said, "look back on this and smile — because it was life and I decided to live it."

Afterword

What follows is Katie's final Facebook post; her last communication to the world at large. She wrote it for her husband Andrew to post after her death. Katie passed away on the morning of August 20th, 2016, lucid, engaged and full of life till the very last moment.

———————

This is Andrew, Katie's husband. It is with deep sadness that I share that Katie succumbed to her cancer this morning. She was surrounded by her family, with her right till the end, and said how at peace with dying she was. She wrote this, to be posted after she died.

"If you are reading this it means that my body has ceased to be of use to me anymore and I have decided it's time to move on. These are the words, the ideas and the thoughts that I would like to leave with you on this occasion.

Please give yourself permission to feel everything you need to feel right now and pretty much always. Cry, scream, dance, whatever strikes you. I mean, I was pretty awesome so I really don't blame you for being pretty dang sad.

But just know that there is no one way, no right way, no better way to "do" grief. However you feel the need to grieve today and in the weeks, months, and years ahead, is good and right.

As you grieve please know that I both loved the hell out of my life and also felt at peace with my passing. Life, like so many things, is much better measured in quality and not quantity and from those standards I lived just about all the life there was to live. I experienced so many wonderful things on this beautiful planet, I had such deep and meaningful love in my life and I got to go on quite an adventure of self-discovery. I truly regret nothing and am grateful for everything. I wouldn't trade my life in, cancer and all, for anything. It's been a great privilege to have lived this spectacular life.

I have a few favors to ask of you: First, please take good care of my husband. It was supposed to be my job but now I must hand it off to you and the universe. He is incredibly capable but please do give him all the space he needs for as long as he lives to grieve in the way he needs and to find a way to live with me in his life in this new way. He has been the best partner, husband, and best friend that I could have asked for. I will never stop loving him and will never stop being in his life. I ask that anyone who loved me, now share your love with him.

Second, please do the same for my parents, my brother and sister-in-law and my closest friends: Meredith and Jacob, the Baeckeroots and everyone else who has been near and dear to me in this life. I have been so lucky to have been raised with such love. I have such wonderful memories of my childhood and I couldn't have asked for more loving parents or a more devoted little brother. I also could not have asked for better friends. They too will find a way to create a new life with this new relationship I will continue to have with them. Please be patient and kind and loving along the way.

Third..."

That was as far as she got. While I'm sure she intended to finish her post, I would suggest that for each person reading, based on your relationship with Katie, fill in the blank for yourself. Katie was so deeply full of love for all of her friends, family, and colleagues, that I know she would want to deliver an honest, loving, and heartfelt individual message to each one of you. We will miss her deeply, and love her forever, and are so thankful for the time we had with her. As she said, it was about quality, not quantity.

Resources

ORGANIZATIONS SUPPORTING YOUNG ADULTS WITH CANCER

First Descents *www.firstdescents.org*

A week-long adventure experience for young adults with cancer.

Stupid Cancer *www.stupidcancer.org*

The largest US-based charity that comprehensively addresses young adult cancer through advocacy, research, support, outreach, awareness, mobile health and social media.

The SAMFund *www.thesamfund.org*

Offering financial support through grants and scholarships to young adults as they transition into their post-treatment lives.

Athletes for Cancer *www.athletes4cancer.org*

Harnesses the healing power of the elements and focuses on renewing, rebuilding, and restarting lives after cancer through outdoor adventure.

Hope for Young Adults with Cancer *www.hope4yawc.org*

Connects young adults with cancer, 18-40, with financial support and a social network.

The Ulman Cancer Fund for Young Adults
www.ulmanfund.org

Supporting, educating and connecting young adults affected by cancer through on-line resources, college scholarships and advocacy.

LiveStrong Foundation *www.livestrong.org*

Offers a comprehensive listing of insurance and financial assistance resources that can help offset the heavy cost burden of a cancer diagnosis.

Patient Advocate Foundation *www.patientadvocate.org*

PAF's scholarship program provides support to young adults under 25 diagnosed with cancer within the past five years.

CancerCare *www.cancercare.org*

Offers assistance for cancer-related costs (home care, child care pain medications) and their professional oncology social workers can help cancer patients find resources.

HealthWell Foundation *www.healthwellfoundation.org*

Fills the gap by helping patients pay their share of prescription drug copayments, deductibles, and health insurance premiums.

Fertile Action *www.fertileaction.org*

Family planning education, advocacy and financial aid (including a pro bono egg-freezing network) for cancer survivors and high-risk patients.

Imerman Angels *www.imermanangels.org*

A "one-on-one cancer support service" that connects a person fighting cancer with a survivor who has beaten the same type of cancer.

True North Treks *www.truenorthtreks.org*

Dedicated to enriching the lives of adolescent and young adult cancer survivors through contemplative and outdoor-based activities.

Cancer and Careers *www.cancerandcareers.org*

Empowers and educates people with cancer to thrive in their workplace.

Re-Mission *www.re-mission.net*

A free 3D shooter video game designed for teens and young adults with cancer.

ORGANIZATIONS SUPPORTING BREAST CANCER

Breast Cancer Action *www.bcaction.org*

Breast Cancer Action's mission is to achieve health justice for all women at risk of and living with breast cancer.

Metavivor *www.metavivor.org*

A non-profit organization dedicated to increasing awareness of advanced breast cancer and equity in research and patient support.

MET UP *www.metup.org*

Committed to changing the landscape of metastatic cancer through direct action.

Young Survival Coalition *www.youngsurvival.org*

An international network of breast cancer survivors and supporters dedicated to the concerns and issues that are unique to young women and breast cancer.

Acknowledgements

I would like to acknowledge Andrew for believing this was worth it all, Rachael and Jenn for saying, "YES!", Angela for agreeing to bring me along for the ride, Liz, Meredith, Lauren, Gail and Cynthia for their thoughtful edits, Mary and Tim for making my Ernest Hemingway dreams come true, Patrick for providing the inspiration and my hundreds of Kickstarter supporters for making this book a reality.

About the Author

KATIE CAMPBELL was a Stage 4 cancer thriver and award-winning writer, speaker and advocate for the young adult cancer movement. She had a passion for connecting with and advocating on behalf of fellow young adult cancer survivors and fighters.

Katie was diagnosed with triple negative breast cancer in the fall of 2013 at the age of 30. After a year of traditional treatments and a few months of remission Katie's cancer returned as Stage 4. Katie was dedicated to fighting her own cancer, going on as many adventures as possible and speaking up about the challenges facing thirty-somethings with cancer.

After her diagnosis, Katie crafted raw and honest accounts of her journey on her own blog, which became a resource to hundreds of cancer fighters. Her writing was also featured by young adult cancer non-profits such as First Descents, Stupid Cancer and Critical Mass.

She shared her own journey as a speaker in a variety of venues including First Descents' annual fundraiser, the Association of Oncology Social Work conference, and the Stupid Cancer podcast. She won the Out Living It Award from First Descents for her inspirational leadership in the young adult cancer movement.

Katie lived with her husband and dog in Frederick, Maryland but loved exploring new countries and cultures whenever she had the chance. She was also an avid rock climber, photographer, graphic designer, and global policy wonk.

Thank You

Thank you so much for coming along on this journey with me. I hope that for you the end of this book is just the beginning of the rest of your big and beautiful life.

To find videos of speeches and presentations I've given on the topics within this book and other resources to help you live your life with courage you can go to:

www.katieacampbell.com/reader-resources

Made in the USA
Middletown, DE
05 June 2017